SILK

*From the Myths & Legends
to the Middle Ages*

Priscilla Lowry

Also by the Author

The Secrets of Silk: From Textiles to Fashion   *The World of Silk*

St John's Press, Auckland
Second Edition 2008

© Priscilla Lowry 2003–2015
First published in the United Kingdom in 2003 by St John's Press, London
Ebook edition 2015
Second Edition St Johns Press, Auckland, New Zealand 2008
Updated 2015
39 Kawerau Avenue, Devonport, Auckland, New Zealand 0624
Email: priscilla.silkroad@gmail.com
Website: www.priscillalowry.co.nz

ISBN 978-0-9941063-2-2

Priscilla Lowry asserts her moral right to be identified as the author of this work.

All rights reserved. No part of this publication may be reproduced or transmitted, in any form or by any means electronic or mechanical, including photocopying, recording, information storage or retrieval system, except for brief reviews, without prior permission in writing from the publishers.

Every effort has been made to contact copyright holders for all images. The author and publisher apologizes for any omissions which they will be pleased to rectify at the earliest opportunity.

A catalogue record for this book is available from the National Library of New Zealand.
Cover illustration: The Lady of the Silkworms.

Contents

Chapter One: Myths and Legends 7

Chapter Two: The Silk Road 25

Chapter Three: Marco Polo 41

Chapter Four: English Medieval Embroidery 65

Chapter Five: The Medieval Silk-women 85

Chapter Six: The Guilds 103

Chapter Seven: Silk in Fashion 123

Chapter Eight: Spinning silk 141

Appendix: 157
Sericulture 158
Silk Routes 162
Marco Polo and Silk 165
Silk Glossary 169
Bibliography 182
Index 190

The Lady of the Silkworms, the mythical Lady Si Ling shi, standing serenely in front of round wicker trays of silkworms feeding on mulberry leaves.

CHAPTER ONE
Myths and Legends

The Lady of the Silkworms

They were lies, all lies, but in ancient times and in a society where the written word was available only to the chosen few, imaginative stories could embroider and flesh out barely understood facts. Myths and legends could hide the truth and keep a secret. Many of the best stories had a beautiful princess, a little magic, an exotic story to tell.

The mythical emperor Fo Xi, 2677–2597 BCE, was believed to have discovered the secrets of silk, but usually Si Ling shi (Lei-tze or Lady Xi-ling) is given the credit. She was the principal wife of the Yellow Emperor, Shih Huang-ti, who ruled China between 259 and 210 BCE. Some Chinese legends say Si Ling shi was really his concubine and other sources say she was his fourteen year old daughter. Most legends describe her as the Lady of the Silkworms or the Goddess of Silk and all agree she was beautiful.

According to the legend, the beautiful princess was walking in the palace gardens with her ladies, and set out under a mulberry tree was a little brazier heating water to make tea. As she passed by, a silk cocoon dropped from the mulberry tree into the bowl of hot water. She picked up a chopstick and as she tried to scoop out the cocoon, she found a single strand of glistening silk attached. As she drew the silk out further and further, she marveled at its length and fineness. She realized then that she had discovered the first secret of silk. It was hot water that dissolved the sericin the gummy substance holding the cocoon and fibres together and now the fibres were free to unwind as a continuous thread. She looked in delight at the fragile shimmering silk and wondered if it could be woven and made into a beautiful soft gown, unique and precious and unlike any garment she had ever worn before. She started to imagine what it would feel like, to be clothed in a cobweb of silken cloth.

Si Ling shi already knew that silkworms ate mulberry leaves; she had seen them on the trees. She knew that they spun a cocoon before turning into a moth that laid eggs that hatched into silkworms. But, until that time, it was not known if the cocoon itself had any value or if the silk could be unwound. One single strand was too thin to be easily managed on its own, but half a dozen cocoons, softened by hot water, could be drawn off together and wound into a skein to dye, weave or transport. The discovery of how to make it into a thicker and more usable thread was the second secret of silk.

This glossy, continuous thread was quite unlike cotton or wool, with its short fibres that needed to be handspun and twisted together to make a usable yarn. Silk was smooth and strong, ideal for weaving into exquisite precious fabrics. Si Ling shi is also credited with the discovery of weaving, but this is unlikely because weaving had already been practiced for many centuries. In ancient China, the Emperor claimed all discoveries, so it is not surprising that the invention of silk weaving was attributed to his wife, the Empress.

Si Ling shi was called the Lady of the Silkworms and honoured with rituals and sacrifices. Court regulations decreed that the Empress and her ladies perform a solemn ceremony to encourage the growing of silk. This ritual was timed to coincide with the fresh spring growth of leaves on the mulberry trees in the third month of the lunar year. The empress and royal concubines prepared themselves by withdrawing from the court, fasting and offering sacrifices. The ladies then rode in horse-drawn carriages in a grand procession to the Temple of the Silkworms on the north-eastern shore of Lake Bei. They were accompanied by thousands of horsemen carrying dragon banners and colourful silk pennons. There is an account of this annual ritual in the Book of Sericulture, the Qin Guan Canshu, written in 1090 CE and also in the Songshu, the Book of the Song

Ladies tending their silkworms, as they feed on mulberry leaves set out on wicker trays.
From T'ien-kung k'ai-wu, by Sung Ying-sing, 1637.

Dynasty (960–1279) which maintains that this complex ritual was first performed in 1119. The ritual and procession continued each year until the fall of the Qing Dynasty in 1911. The Hall of Imperial Silkworms with the Altar of Silkworms was situated within the Forbidden City, and this area called Beihei, is now a children's park.

Some Chinese communities have their own folk tales to explain the origin of silk. The people of Sichuan honoured a god-king called Cancong who distributed several thousand golden silkworms to his people. Cancong means 'a silkworm cluster' and his subjects believed they were the first to wear silk. He apparently always wore green, and is known as 'the god in green'.

The State Secret

Sericulture is the name given to the different processes in the cultivation of silk. The discovery of how to unwind silk from the cocoon and use the thread for weaving precious fabrics was of immense importance to the Empire, so controls were quickly put in place to ensure that the secret remained within the court. There is very little reliable documentation of this early period but it seems that the key was to keep each part of the process separate, so that no one knew the whole story. The provinces around the Yangzte Basin had the perfect climate for growing mulberry trees, the *morus alba* and the tiny indigenous silkworm, the *Bombyx mandarina Moore*. Sericulture was established there and the local people learnt to care for and cherish their silkworms.

Hand-reeling the silk from the cocoons being soaked in bowls of hot water to make a useable fibre.
From T'ien-kung k'ai-wu, by Sung Ying-sing, 1637.

By royal decree at the end of each season, the cocoons were collected, bundled up into large sacks and transported to another district. There the villagers looked forward to the arrival of the cocoons, and the work and income they represented. They boiled the cocoons to free the silk fibre from the gummy sericin and reeled and tied the silk into skeins. Sometimes the thread was 'thrown', which twisted the fibres together to make them stronger and more resilient. These people only knew about reeling, throwing and skeining silk, not of how the silk came to be on the cocoon. The skeins were packaged into fardels or bundles and once again sent vast distances to be dyed, or to major weaving centres like Sichuan. The very best silk was sent to the court itself.

Within the court was the gynaeceum or women's weaving workshop, where highly skilled weavers wove the best silk into beautiful fabrics for the use of the Emperor and court. One select group of women came from a long line of court weavers and commanded the highest esteem, because they alone knew the secret skills of weaving the cryptic and mysterious pattern known as the Sacred Eye. The knowledge of this particular technique had been jealously guarded and handed down from mother to daughter through many generations.

The people of each district only understood their particular aspect of sericulture. Hundreds of miles away, other villagers dealt with another part of the preparation of silk, so no one actually knew the whole story of how silk was made. There were heavy fines and penalties given to those who betrayed the secrets of silk, and great pressure was put on everyone associated with sericulture to ensure that the secrets were kept within the Middle Kingdom. In the villages and hamlets, gruesome folk-tales were told and retold, of spies caught trading the secrets of silk. There was also another method of punishment to ensure that no one spread the secrets. It was called decapitation.

The traditional date for the discovery of silk is 2640 BCE, but China began cultivating and domesticating silk long before that. In one archaeological site, the outline of a silkworm, probably the tiny indigenous *Bombyx mandarina Moore*, was found carved into a little ivory cup, thought to be between 6000 and 7000 years old. Over the centuries, these primitive native silkworms were gradually superseded by the larger and more productive strain, the *Bombyx mori*. In 1927 on a Neolithic site, 7000–1500 BCE, in Shanxi Province in Northern China, a *Bombyx mori* cocoon dated between 2600 and 1300 BCE was found, deliberately cut in half, indicating that someone had actually handled it.

In recent years there have been some exciting discoveries of ancient textiles, like the little bundle of red silk ribbons and woven fragments, found at Qianshanyang in Zhejiang. They were carbon dated to around 3000 BCE and seem to be one of the earliest actual examples of woven *Bombyx mori* silk. A bamboo basket containing scraps of woven silk was discovered in the ancient silk-growing district of Wu-hsing in Chekiang. Silk was used as wadding for winter garments and quilted bedding and one fragment of quilted silk taffeta has been dated to around 2800 BCE. During the Shang Dynasty, c1600–1027 BCE, silk wrapping cloths were used as part of burial rituals to wrap precious bronze and jade funereal items. The weave left an imprint or pseudomorph on the vessel as the silk decayed, and the ghost of the pattern can still be seen under special conditions.

Spindles and other spinning and weaving accessories have been found in sites along the lower Yangtze River, but not looms or large pieces of equipment. Early looms were primitive affairs, with wooden cross members and a strap worn around the weaver's back. They were not large wooden structures like more recent looms, but simple pieces of wood and string and rather fragile. They could be rolled up and transported, but just as easily damaged and subject to decay, and so have not survived. All these discoveries help to confirm that sericulture was not only practiced in China from a very early date, but that the people had a sophisticated knowledge of the processes of unwinding the cocoons, throwing, dyeing, weaving, quilting and sewing.

The word for silk was incorporated into the written language, the characters sometimes woven into the silks. Jin, the Chinese word for brocade, has been found woven into the borders of a number of polychrome silk compound-weave fabrics, dated to 1100 BCE. Silk quilts, gowns and burial cloths from around 300 BCE have been found in a Chu tomb in the Hubei Province. The workmanship is exquisite, the colours well-preserved and many have designs showing

Weaving silk on a large upright loom.
From T'ien-kung k'ai-wu, by Sung Ying-sing, 1637.

flowers, swirling clouds and quaint stylized animals. Some decorative patterns are based on the shape of the silkworm or the cocoon. These early finds are just the first glimmers of a developing silk industry.

Some of the earliest writing, in the form of pictograms on oracle bones, date from the Shang dynasty, 1600 to 1027 BCE. By 300 BCE the actual words for silk, mulberry and silkworms are found inscribed on ancient shell and bronze articles. Silk paper is mentioned in early Chinese texts and examples were found in a refuse site at Yamen near the Jade Gate, by the nineteenth century explorer Sir Marc Aurel Stein. These include a strip of white silk, written in Kharoshthi script which offers an early proof that silk was used for writing on, either before or in preference to paper. Among many other examples are two fragments of a letter from an officer named Zheng. He was stationed on the northern frontier and was writing to recommend a colleague to an officer garrisoned at Dunhuang.

Paper was initially made from rags and bark, but in 105 CE, Ts'ai Lun discovered that if short lengths of silk fibre were added during the pulp stage, they gave strength and durability to the paper. Between 100 BCE and 300 CE, everyday information was written on cheap, wood or bamboo slips that were scraped clean and reused. To ensure security, these narrow slips were tied and sealed with a layer of clay and stamped with the official's seal, or the clerk's 'chop'. Woven silk fabric was preferred for the exquisite silk text rolls of the emperor's personal library. These sacred and literary texts, found in graves in Central China, contain information on magic and mysticism and many are special presentation copies of maps, diagrams and treaties on astrology and medicine.

Gradually the knowledge and practice of sericulture spread throughout China; from Hainan in the south to Heilungkiang in the north, from Shantung in the east to Khotan in the west. Sericulture was established in Gansu province, where tomb bricks were painted with scenes of people picking mulberry leaves, silkworm breeding and silk weaving. The southern province of Chengdu, the ancient capital of Sichuan became so famous for its fine silk weaving that it was known as 'Brocade City'. The north-eastern provinces of

Tomb Bricks from Xincheng, 20 km NW of Jiayuguan. A boy stands on guard to scare away predators while a man collects either mulberry leaves or silkworm cocoons from off the tree.
China Travel and Tourism Press.

Shantung and Liaoning became centres for shantung and pongee silks, made from the silk of wild tussah silkworms. They require a temperate climate and these wild tussah silks have been produced from the time of the Han and Wei dynasties.

Gifts, Tribute and Trade

Gorgeous, colourful, decorative and precious woven silks made desirable and prestigious tribute gifts. In Shu Ching's history of the Chinese philosopher Confucius, dated after 500 BCE, the Chinese Emperor, the Great Yu, 2205–2197 BCE, demanded and got tribute gifts. The Book of Annuak specifically mentions lengths of blue and red silk as gifts from six provinces.

The word 'gift' is rather a misnomer. The Chinese system of gift and tribute was a subtle and highly sophisticated balance, reflecting both quality and quantity of the gifts offered and the power and status of the people involved. The Emperor was believed to be the Son of Heaven, heir to the Middle Kingdom. All people were subordinate to him, bowed down and honoured him. On arrival, the visiting envoy made his offering of valuable gifts. The Emperor then gave orders for beautiful silks and other costly items to be assembled, to present to the envoy in exchange. The gifts were accepted with a great profusion of thanks and acknowledgement of obligation. The Emperor saw the gifts as a rightful tribute from a lesser to a greater power. To the envoy it was probably just trade by another name and so the balance of power was seen to be maintained. The envoy returned to his own country taking bolts of silk with him, but not the knowledge of sericulture. In this way, silk fabric, along with many other items, passed out of China.

In ancient times the Chinese court rarely engaged in trade with other nations because it saw itself as superior and self-sufficient. Silk was the most unique and highly desired of any product, the envy of every other nation. It was not however, looked on as a source of income for the treasury because it was much simpler to just threaten the people and demand that they pay higher taxes. The court controlled the production and collection of silk so it was used as a gift to reward people. Like any commodity, it varied enormously in quality, colour, texture and the complexity of the weave. Each bolt of fabric was carefully graded and then allocated, following a set scale, to the person of the appropriate rank in the hierarchy. It was even used as a negotiable currency and state servants, officials and soldiers could be paid in cash or lengths of silk. One officer serving on the North West Frontier was given two rolls of silk to the value of 900 coins as his month's pay. Eventually silk turned up in the marketplace as an item of trade or exchange. By the time of the Han Dynasty, 206 BCE–220 CE, lengths of silk cloth, bags of cocoons or bundles of silk floss could replace money and constitute part of a farmer's payment of taxes.

Sericulture was so widely practiced that silk became one of the recognized products used to fulfill one's tax obligations. In the seventh century, Yo was a handcraft or local product tax of 3%, which every able-bodied male between the ages of twenty-two and sixty was required to pay. Zoyo or corvee labour was another form of tax, requiring each male to work for ten days each year on a government project like road building. To avoid being conscripted, the farmer could offer 26 feet or 7.9 metres of cloth, silk floss or another local product in lieu of his labour. Cho was also a local tax paid to the Imperial Court, initially levied on each household. Eventually everyone was required to pay it in the form of rough silk, thread, silk floss, cloth, iron or salt. The only people exempt were those on military service. Each family had the responsibility to transport these products to the capital, and to pay for food and accommodation while they were there. It was an enormous burden on the peasants and they complained and resorted to every subterfuge to evade these taxes. By the tenth century, the central authority was breaking down and these taxes were often surreptitiously diverted into the coffers of the tax collectors and powerful officials.

Silk Spreads from China

No secret can be kept forever and with wars, trade and the passage of missionaries and adventurers, the secrets of silk gradually made their way east to Korea and Japan and northwest across the Eurasian Steppes to Russia and south into India. Some of the oldest written references to Indian woven silk are in the sacred epics and Sanskrit

Climbing trees to collect mulberry leaves, usually the responsibility of the men and boys in the family.
Bibliotheque Nationale, Paris.

texts, in the Ramayana and the Mahabharata. India had its own indigenous wild tussah silk moths, but the cultivation of a domestic variety of white silk was in the future.

Exciting stories abound of how the knowledge of sericulture spread around the world, stories rich in wars, espionage and mayhem. Sometime before 200 BCE, Chinese silk workers went to Korea, possibly not voluntarily as emigrants but as slaves, captured in war and made to work. There is evidence that during the early Mahan period in Korea, the Puyo people were wearing patterned silk clothes. Silk fabrics dated from 28 BCE have been found in Japan, but the knowledge of sericulture took longer to spread throughout the islands. Japanese chronicles tell of how a Chinese prince and his household were exiled, possibly for some misdemeanor, and sought asylum in Japan, taking a real risk by bringing silkworm eggs with them as a gift. According to the Nihon Shoki chronicle, the Japanese government encouraged sericulture and collected silk as taxes as early as the fifth century. A temple was erected in the province of Sethu to these pioneer silk weavers, and the industry grew into one of national importance.

There are a number of different versions of one of the best-loved stories of how silk reached Khotan on the furthest borders of Western China. A Tibetan legend of around 400 CE described how, as a token of his fidelity and veneration, the King of Khotan, sometimes known as Vijaya Jaya, petitioned the Chinese Emperor for the hand of a princess of the royal house. In her grief at leaving her family and going so far away without even the comfort of silk gowns and quilts, she decided to take a terrible risk and take both mulberry seeds and silkworm eggs hidden in her headdress. At the border the guards searched the whole caravan, but Princess Punyesvara was not searched; she passed through the gates into Khotan and the knowledge of sericulture reached the far western territories. This version of the legend says she did not tell the King she had brought the silkworm eggs with her so when they hatched, the King's ministers accused her of breeding 'little poisonous snakes' and demanded that they be burnt. She was distraught at the thought of losing them after all the risks she had taken, but she managed to save a few and after they had spun their cocoons she showed the silk to the King. He quickly understood the importance of silk to her, and the priceless value to his kingdom of establishing sericulture.

A similar story was told in the history of the T'ang, the Tangshu, by the travelling Buddhist monk Hsuan Tsang, 602–664 CE. China had only recently been re-unified under the T'ang dynasty and the King of Khotan heard rumours that silk existed in the east. He coveted this precious textile and sent a delegation to the Emperor T'ai-tsung to ask for a bride from the emperor's family and this was granted. The King's second request for silkworm eggs was forcibly denied and the emperor had the border stations closely watched. Princess Wen-ch'eng decided to risk severe punishment by hiding the silkworm eggs in her clothing when she passed out of China and into Khotan. To celebrate her first successful batch of cocoons, she had an inscription carved in stone which said: 'It is prohibited to kill the silkworm. Only when the moth has left the cocoon may the silk be used.' In this version, silk could not be unreeled from the whole cocoon because the moth had made a hole through which to escape which broke the silk filament. This suggests that the silk fibre was spun in short lengths rather than reeled as a continuous thread.

Khotan flourished during the T'ang dynasty, but it is hard to tell from the stories the real extent of silk production. During excavations in 1914 in the desert near Dandan-Oilik, Sir Marc Aurel Stein found an ancient painting of a princess with a basket on her head of what looks like cocoons. Nearby a girl is pictured weaving, while another girl points to the princess's hair. This may illustrate the legend and it helps to confirm that the knowledge of sericulture had already spread to Khotan.

The Spread of Silk to the West

In the West, although it was not known how silk was made, there are many mentions of it in classical literature and wonderful misunderstandings and theories as to its origin. Alexander the Great's teacher Aristotle, 384–322 BCE, mentions silk in his writings in 'Hist. anim,' V19 (17) 11. He describes the silkworm as a 'curious horned worm'. He credits a Phoenician princess, Pamphile, daughter of Plateus, on the island of Cos off the coast of Turkey, with the discovery of silk and describes the fabric she wove as 'woven wind'. The island of Cos produced an inferior wild silk, but Aristotle obviously valued it. Pliny, 23–79 CE, was a Roman historian and he agreed with him, and was convinced that silk grew on trees, saying in his Natural History (IV.54) that '. . . the Seres are famous for the wool from their forests. They remove the down from the leaves with the help of water', so he got it partly right, but clearly he had not had firsthand experience of sericulture. Virgil, 70–19 BCE, also describes how '. . . the Chinese comb off leaves their delicate down . . .' Flax and cotton are both vegetable fibres, widely known in classical times, so Pliny and Virgil probably expected silk to come from a similar source.

The Bible also has at least four references to silk. In the book of Ezekiel, written around 300 BCE, in Chapter 16, verse 10, it says 'I clothed thee also in broidered work and shod thee with badger's skin and girded thee about with fine linen and covered thee with silk,' and in verse 13: 'Thus wast thou decked with gold and silver and thy raiment too was of fine linen and silk and broidered work.' In the Book of Proverbs it says, ' She maketh herself coverings of tapestry: her clothing is silk and purple.' Even in biblical times, silk was known and valued and considered most precious.

There is also a Babylonian legend told by Ovid, 43 BCE–17 CE, in his *Metamorphosis*. It is a real Romeo and Juliet story, the one Shakespeare retells as a comic piece in his *Midsummer Night's Dream*. Ovid's story tells how Pyramus and Thisbe, when their parents refused to allow them to marry, arranged to meet secretly under a mulberry tree. Disaster struck when Thisbe, who arrived first, was frightened by a lion who grabbed her scarf. The lion had recently killed an ox and when Pyramus found the scarf covered in blood but no Thisbe, he believed that the lion had attacked and killed her and he killed himself. Thisbe found Pyramus dead and killed herself, which is why, legend says, the white mulberry tree has black fruit, which drips blood red juice. These imaginative stories certainly added to the romance and mystery of silk.

Beautiful silk textiles gradually became more readily available in Central Asia and Persia. The Persians quickly established themselves as the sole middlemen between East and West, but then war broke out between Byzantium and Persia, and the west was cut off from its supply of silk. In Byzantium, Emperor Justinian I, c482–565 CE, had his capital and power base at Constantinople. He was one of the most brilliant and ablest of leaders, but he had become increasingly anxious as his prosperous and pleasure-loving people squandered their money on luxuries and in particular on gorgeous imported silks. Two-thirds of the Byzantine Empire's treasury went on imports of luxury items from the East. High court and church dignitaries dressed lavishly in silk, emblazoned with imperial purple insignia. The wealthy people paraded in the finest silk robes and were buried in silk winding sheets.

Justinian had a real problem keeping his people focused on the

Justinian at the moment when the two Nestorian monks hand him the hollow cane containing the silkworm eggs.
Karel de Mallery, engravings of sericulture in Europe, in Collection of the Dutch Textile Museum, Tilburg, The Netherlands.

priorities. There was a cavalier attitude to the necessity of holding a treasure chest and being prepared for the serious business of war. If silk could be produced locally, then trade would no longer have to go through Persia and other nations who demanded exorbitant bribes and taxes. Further, the quantity and price of this luxury item could be controlled by the Byzantine state. The collection of a local tax on silk would not come amiss, either. A little international espionage was called for, as the knowledge of sericulture was still a closely guarded secret denied to the west.

Two travelling Nestorian monks saw an opportunity and obtained an audience with Justinian and convinced him that they could bring him the secrets of silk. There is some doubt as to whether the monks went to China or Northern India to get the silkworm eggs. Procopius of Caesarea, who died 562 CE, said that the monks had spent time in a country called Serinda, an early name for China, where the silkworm eggs were covered with dung, to keep them warm. (War of the Goths, IV, 17). The sixth century Roman

Princess in Khotan. Marc Aurel Stein identified the picture of the girl in the tomb painting as the Princess, as she seems to have cocoons hidden in her headdress. Another girl nearby points to her head, possibly reinforcing the story.
British Museum.

chronicler Theophanes maintained they went to India and the journey to get the silkworm eggs took two years. On their return in 552 CE the two dusty, travel-worn monks were taken into Justinian's presence. They bowed deeply and then up-ended their hollow cane walking sticks. Out tumbled mulberry seeds and tightly rolled twists of paper with the tiny silkworm eggs attached. The eggs had been kept cool during the journey, waiting for the warmth of spring when they would hatch out. The monks were suitably rewarded and given every assistance to get sericulture established. Imperial workshops were set up by the church and state to try to monopolize and control production. These were also known as gynaeceum, but this time staffed by both men and women. Despite royal backing, the quantities of silk required by the citizens of Byzantium were far more than the new industry could support and silk still had to be imported. But, as in China, no secret can be kept forever. The knowledge of sericulture was dispersed, and the European silk industry developed from these beginnings.

Names for Silk

There is a long history of confusion about the names for China and silk. Some people called China, Sinae or Thinae, the Greeks and Romans called it Seres or Serica. The Roman writer Cosmas Indicopleusts, early in the sixth century CE, when he mentions China, calls it Tzinista, but he was not too sure and concluded that '. . . further than Tzinista, there is neither navigation nor an inhabited land.' Sanskrit writings also refer to Cina, from the name for the Qin dynasty, from which China is derived, Qin being in the north and Cathay being in the south. According to Theophanus of Byzantium, c750–817 CE, sericulture was introduced by a Persian who came from the land of Seres. The name possibly comes from ser, the central Asian word for yellow, the colour associated with the Chinese Imperial court. Every country has its own word for silk: The Chinese call it Si, South China used See or Szu, the Koreans Soi, and the nomads of Central Asia called it Sir, Sirghe or Sirkek. The Jews sometimes call their exquisite silk fabric Sherikoth, while the Arabs called it Saraqa. In the west the Latin texts use Sericum, French Soie, German Seide and English Silk.

A village on the Silk Road through the high mountains in northern Pakistan. The harsh conditions are obvious in the narrow tracks high on the barren scree and rock slopes above the Indus River.

CHAPTER TWO
The Silk Road

Central Asia has always been a challenge to those who tried to cross it. It extends for over 5000 miles, from the Black Sea via the Hindu Kush and the High Pamirs, across the vast Taklamakan and the Gobi deserts. Much of it is wasteland, harsh and inhospitable.

It has deep craters and waterless ancient riverbeds and is partly ringed by soaring snow-covered mountains. Very occasionally it is temperate and gentle, a glimpse of heaven. From time immemorial, people have tried to control and conquer this ancient land. Whole nations have swept in, fighting, pillaging and claiming their right to be there and possess. Others have sought new pastures for their herds and new markets for their goods. Gradually over the last 5000 years, a cobweb of shifting trails to summer grazing lands, strings of watering holes and passes through high mountains have been established.

These tracks serviced traders and bandits, soldiers and government officials, tough resilient men able to withstand the violent, extreme changes in climate and terrain and to protect themselves and their goods. Over the centuries Buddhists, Manichaeans, Zoroastrians, Confucians, Taoists, Muslims, Jews and Christians have journeyed thousands of miles to seek enlightenment and proclaim their message. Even more effective at spreading ideas than the official missionaries were the unofficial ones, the traders along the roads. The routes were a conduit for new ideas, new technology, new agricultural methods and sericulture. The Silk Route is the collective name for some of these patterns of travel, not one road, but a network of shifting tracks. It had no name at all until Baron Ferdinand von Richthofen (1833–1905), the German geographer and traveller, wrote his major work on China, *Aufgaben der Geographie* in 1883. There he coined the phrase, *die Seidenstrassen*, the Silk Road.

Caravanserai, offering accommodation and shelter for the men and stabling for their animals, grew up around wells and at crossroads. There the men rested, replenished their supplies, acquired fresh pack animals, hired guides and traded their silk. Markets evolved, selling jewels, spices, medicines and slaves, any commodity that would turn a profit. The men travelled in groups for security, transporting the goods from one oasis or trading centre to another and then trading on. The High Pamirs formed a natural barrier so it was rare for Chinese merchants to go as far as Rome, or Romans to Ch'ang-an.

Caravanserai, where a camel waits patiently at the abandoned desert city of Gaochang.

For a time, some routes would be favoured, the travellers welcomed, engaged in trade and helped on their way. Then the political regime changed and as cities were razed to the ground and lands conquered, new rulers imposed their wills. A harsh or greedy administration made the route too difficult, the bribes and taxes too high, the defenses too strong, so a new way had to be found.

Changes in weather patterns and terrain stopped people from crossing boundaries. The violent, whirling sand storm known as the kara buran, buried whole cities. Oases dried up and the salt flats took over where once there had been vegetation and fresh water to feed the travellers and their animals.

Trade along the Silk Road

All the various prerequisites of trade were set up along the silk routes including mints to produce a dependable and valid coinage. The Macedonian merchant Maes Titianus produced a travellers' guide. He did not travel, but his agents returned with information about the actual routes, services and conditions and colourful stories about Sera Metropolis, the City of Silk, probably Ch'ang-an, and Sinae Metropolis, possibly Loyang. Letters survive from traders from the second century BCE. They had to be cleared through a merchants' organization called the Karum and often state 'you are my brother' or 'you are my father', indicating that the person was an agent trading on their behalf, aware of their requirements and preferences. Wherever there were men with a sense of adventure and purpose, a lust for life and riches, there you would find silk. Silk was a high profit item, relatively easy to transport and always in high demand. Providing the taxes and bribes were paid, the goods got through, despite governments, wars or lack of a common language.

The usual language of trade was Aramaic, especially in the lowlands. The 'koine' or common language gradually replaced Aramaic, while in the highlands, Persian was the norm. Trade was not necessarily conducted in an organized manner. Some people used a secret, 'silent trade' system, later described in the first century by Pomponius Mela in his *'Chorography'*. At an agreed site, goods were displayed and the trader left so that another could lay his goods for exchange, beside them. There was much adding and subtracting of items until a balance was achieved. Then each trader came and claimed his exchanged goods and departed, often without actually meeting or speaking a word. Sometimes it was not the lack of language but the need for secrecy that led to another form of 'silent trade'. Here the traders would meet and clasp each other's hand within their wide sleeves. The traders' inscrutable, weathered faces gave nothing away as they tapped out the prices and conditions on each other's palm until a deal was agreed. The transaction terms were arranged and finalized without curious onlookers ever discovering the details.

By the second century BCE, the Kushan Empire had conquered Bactria which lay at the meeting point of the great trading routes: the road south to India, the Silk Road linking China with Parthian Iran and Roman Syria, and the road to the Black Sea which went north of the Caspian Sea and the Caucasus Mountains. The Parthians on the wide Iranian Plateau established their vast territory straddling the Silk Road, and very quickly realized that great profits could be made by controlling the Western section of the route and demanding the payment of taxes and bribes. The Chinese too, soon set up commercial and political links, and a Chinese chronicle dated 106 BCE recorded what was believed to be the first major caravan from China to An-hsi, Parthia, and the Iranian Plateau. By 60 BCE the Chinese controlled both the southern and northern routes of the Eastern sector of the Silk Road. The trader Pan Ch'iao wrote to his brother Pan Ku, saying ' I now send 300 pieces of white silk which I want you to trade for Bactrian horses, some rugs and (the aromatic) storax '. The domination by the two Empires, the Han in the East and the Persian to the West, helped to ensure peace and security on the route and trade flourished.

By now China had developed a practical foreign policy and was in effect happy to trade. However, it still retained the fictions of 'tribute'

The Great Wall is usually made of local materials and here at Jiayuguan its is made of layers of reeds and hard compacted loess from the surrounding Gobi desert.

A Bactrian camel, with its fardels of silk as depicted in Matthew Paris' map of the Holy Land in his *Chronica majora*.
With permission of the Master and Fellows of Corpus Christi College Cambridge.

and 'gifts', which fitted its vision of itself as a civilizing society and the Confucian ideal of order and Imperial Virtue. Large quantities of silk were increasingly used in exchange for tribute, to enforce control and compliance from neighbouring states. It was also used to pay soldiers' wages and for other services, so some silk was traded on. This policy, largely based on silk, did stimulate commercial activity, but it was financially ruinous to the Han economy. The annals carefully record all gifts and exchanges. In 51 BCE China gave Huhanxie, a suzerain from one of the neighbouring territories, seventy-seven sets of bedcovers and two years later the same again, plus 110 sets of clothing. Later records mention other gifts totalling 8000 pieces of embroidered silk and 6000 pounds of silk floss. Fifty years later, these gifts had expanded to 84,000 pieces of embroidered silk and 78,000 pounds of silk floss. Yu Ying-shih calculated that the system absorbed seven per cent of the total revenue of the Empire, excluding military and administrative expenses. Naturally, some men tried to take advantage of the system and made false claims. In 166 CE a merchant arrived in Tonkin from Rome saying he was an emissary from the Roman Emperor Marcus Aurelius Antoninius, but he was found out and discredited.

It became an extensive two-way traffic. It was estimated that there were at least twelve great caravans a year of camels, men and goods. Furs came from Russia, ivory from India and jade from Central Asia, which was especially highly valued by the Chinese. Pearls and gems flowed west to Antioch, Damascus and the coastal cities. China exported to the western regions vast quantities of silk, skeins of yarn and bolts of cloth, the finest coming from the Imperial Workshops. Exquisite Chinese fabrics from the Han and later T'ang dynasties have been discovered in burial sites along these routes. The colours still glow and many feature embroideries using satin and knot stitches, quilting and fine applique work. The Chinese had a fascination with all things western so woollens, linens, coral, amber, lacquer and glass were transported overland to China. Glassmaking was first developed in Sidon around the first century BCE and was highly valued as it was not manufactured in China until the fifth century CE. Cinnamon bark, spices and rhubarb, desired for their for medicinal purposes, were traded along the route as were military items, bronze and iron, asbestos, mirror and ostriches which the Chinese called 'camel birds'. They believed all these wonderful items came from Da Qin, Great Rome, their name for the Roman Empire. The Romans simply called their territory *'orbis terrarum'* or 'The World'. It was still a very unequal trade; there was far more silk going west than other items going east.

Silk in the West

Territories are won and empires expanded through success in war, and trade follows. After Alexander the Great's death in 323 BCE, Ptolemy I, c367–283 BCE, claimed Egypt as his portion of the vast empire. The capital Alexandria soon became wealthy, and fairs and centres for artisans were established because it was effectively the western end of the spice route from India to Egypt. Silk fabrics have been found buried in the graves of some of the bandits who preyed on travellers along the route so it was clearly used for transporting silk to the Mediterranean. The opulent silks captured the imagination of the luxury loving Egyptians and they called China Serica, the Land of Silk. Cleopatra, 69–30 BCE, the last ruler of the Ptolemaic line in Egypt, exploited the exotic and alluring qualities of silk and the ravishing, diaphanous silks she wore certainly made her ministers nervous and contributed to her reputation as a temptress.

The largest share of Alexander's former Empire was claimed, then governed by the first Seleucid, Seleucus Nicator, c358–280 BCE. The area included Persia, Afghanistan, Bactria, Syria, Mesopotamia and Armenia. Seleucus knew that silk would bring prestige and wealth to his nation, and the control of it increase his own power, so he tried to direct the silk trade towards the seaport of Antioch, one of the western focal points of the Silk Road. Later, the city gave its name to Antioch cloth, a type of figured silk brocade, patterned with birds, whose heads, beaks and feet were picked out in gold. Another equally important city, Seleucia, was built on the banks of the Tigris near the decaying city of Babel and it became the main Mesopotamian crossroad city for the silk trade.

There is something exotic and mysterious about silk, so it often features in fables and tales of battles and acts of daring and courage. The appearance of vibrantly coloured silk banners at the Battle of Carrhae near the Euphrates River in 53 BCE influenced the outcome of an important battle and the course of history. The powerful, opposing Parthian archers, banners aloft, came thundering down towards the Roman legions led by Marcus Licinius Crassus, the Governor of Syria. The Romans had never seen such dazzling colours; they panicked, broke ranks and fled at the sight of the advancing cavalcade. The triumphant Parthians gloried in their success, yet within ten years and peace at last between the Romans and the Parthians, similar banners were flying all over Rome, this time in honour of Julius Caesar, back from one of his triumphant campaigns.

Silk was still scarce and expensive, but the Roman citizens wanted their share of the luxuries of life. The richest and most powerful Romans wore only small pieces of silk, circles, strips or squares, sewn onto their toga and tunics. These silk fragments were the insignia of power, the mark of a patrician, especially when they were dyed purple or embroidered with gold or silver thread. Gradually, fine silk fabrics became more readily available, but still at a price. Those people who saw themselves as leaders, politically, economically or socially, sought to display their wealth, taste and power by wearing the latest fashion. The Roman philosopher Seneca, 5BCE –65CE, became gravely concerned at the display of sparkling, translucent silks. He wrote, 'I see silken clothes, if one can call them clothes at all, that in no degree afford protection either to the body or the modesty of the wearer, and clad in which no woman could honestly swear she is not naked.'

The Roman Emperor Tiberius, 14–37 CE, around the same time as Seneca, also tried to shame his subjects from wearing silk, saying it 'confuse men with women' (Annals III 53). Tacitus in his Annals II 33 forbade men to 'disgrace themselves by wearing of silk materials', but in reality, it made no difference at all.

Pliny, 23–79 CE, also became critical of the way '. . . a lady would appear in public in transparent dress'. He went on to say '. . . they unravel the heavy silk fabrics and re-weave them into shimmering gauzes, known as 'glass togas' and it is through such difficult work that our women form the double task of separating the strands and reweaving them'. Pliny had only a limited understanding of sericulture and weaving, as he still thought silk grew on trees, so he probably did not fully understand just how difficult it would be to unravel silk fabrics, split the thicker threads into finer ones and reweave them. Loosely woven, poor quality fabric will fray, and the fine threads often break and become tangled and useless for reweaving, although short broken threads can be incorporated in tapestry weaving. Silk fibre was imported into Rome in both skeins and bundles, as well as bolts of cloth, and could have been woven locally, to the current requirements of the fashion conscious citizens. Light-weight plain weave fabric is relatively simple to produce, but the exotic, rich silks would still have been imported at vast expense.

Men continued to deck themselves out in the most brilliant silks, many squandering a fortune, to the extent that the Roman Emperor Vespasian, 69–79 CE, became extremely worried by the enormous quantities of precious silks being imported and the consequent outpouring of gold bullion from the treasury. Pliny maintained that one hundred million sesterces were transferred each year in trade with India, Arabia and other countries, much for the purchase of silk.

In the West there was still no clear idea about the origin of silk and many educated men tried to offer an explanation. In the

Boccaccio, from *De claris mulieribus*, shows lady picking silk cocoons off mulberry bushes. The artist knew the story of Pamphile discovering silk on the Island of Cos, but had little understanding that it was the silkworm not the cocoon that had legs and ate mulberry leaves.
Fol. 69, Bibliotheque Nationale, Paris.

second century CE, the Greek geographer and historian Pausanias no longer accepted Pliny's statement that silk was plant-based and that 'The first men who were involved in it were the Seres, famous for the wool of their forests.' Pausanias would have been aware of the legends of Pamphile, the daughter of Plateus who was said to have discovered silk on the Greek island of Cos, but he was not at all clear on every point. In his *'Description of Greece'* (VI, 26), he maintains that silk came from a little animal that the Greeks called 'Ser'. The rest is fantasy because he described the animal as being twice the size of a scarab and resembling the spiders that made their webs in the trees. He described how these silk spiders had eight legs around which they wrapped the fine thread. They lived in cages and the Seres fed them millet seed for the first four years and then during the fifth year, gave them a green reed to eat until they burst. He then stated categorically that the best silk was inside the corpse where the greater part of the thread was found. It was an imaginative explanation, but as he was an educated and widely travelled man, and there was already wild silk in Greece, it was all rather farfetched.

A Time of Change

With drought conditions increasing during the early years of the first century CE, the nomadic people of the Asian Steppes were on the move seeking better pastures for their herds. They struck terror in the hearts of the vulnerable villagers by their strength and number, as they ranged across the land. The Roman, Bactrian and Chinese Empires were beginning to decline, yet the Parthians continued to prosper because the most viable route was through their territory. From the time of Augustus Caesar, 63 BCE–14 CE, the main routes across Central Asia had been relatively safe and well organized, but financially punitive because of the bribes and taxes demanded en route.

As a result, both East and West looked to expand their seaborne foreign trade. It was organized into several stages using a combination of sea and land routes, depending on the season and weather, and the likelihood of being attacked by pirates. Persian ships would go to Canton in China then back via Malaya and India, bringing silks and spices. Some Chinese silk went overland to Alexandria and the Phoenician cities, now in present day Lebanon, to be dyed and woven before being shipped on to Rome and other ports in Europe. By this time the monsoon was known to Indian and Arab sailors, but not in the West, so it was not until 50 CE that a Greek captain from Egypt started using the monsoon winds to sail directly from the Red Sea ports to India. Navigation was still difficult so sailors followed the coastline by day and took their bearings from the stars by night. As knowledge of the seas increased, Romans began to transport men and merchandise by sea, thus avoiding the Parthians altogether.

In Rome, the trade in silk continued to flourish despite official disapproval and by 380 CE, a Roman historian noted peevishly that silk 'once confined to the nobility, now spread to all classes without distinction, even to the lowest'. The wearing of silk was a way of indicating a person's status within society, an outward and visible sign of wealth, power and refinement, and without these distinctions it was hard to tell who was important. Some of the most luxurious silk was worth its weight, ounce for ounce in gold, its cost having increased by up to forty times. These imported silks were exquisitely woven, with complex patterns, embroidered and encrusted with jewels and dyed using the most costly means. All manner of people, aristocrats, clerics and merchants, as well as fashionable women, were abandoning their simpler styles and wearing sophisticated silk clothes. Silk had taken Rome by storm.

Rome still had to pay for its silk in gold, with serious consequences for the economy. Rome had been in gradual decline since around 200 CE and the financial impact on the treasury of importing vast quantities of silk was a significant contributor to Rome's downfall. Gold was pouring from the treasury to pay for the luxuries demanded by its citizens. When the Visigoths (376–410) had Rome under siege, their leader Almaric demanded and got from the city a ransom which included 5000 pounds of gold, 30,000 pounds of silver and 4000 silk tunics.

The Persians continued to control silk crossing the Iranian Plateau. Rome was the major silk supplier to Western Europe so to their mutual benefit, they negotiated a commercial agreement naming the Persian silk city of Nisibus in Iranian Mesopotamia as the official centre for purchasing silk for the West. Christianity was spreading and one branch, the Nestorians, set up a theological college in Nisibus. Constantine's, 274–337 CE, conversion to what became Orthodox Christianity, gave it official status in the Byzantine Empire. Prodigious quantities of luxurious silks were

Chinese ship with both sails and oars, with archers and men on the lookout for pirates.

required and the churches shimmered and glowed with silken hangings, heavily embroidered with gold and silver. Silk was used for liturgical vestments for the clergy and winding cloths for the dead. Within a short space of time there were five guilds in his capital city Constantinople, trading or working exclusively in silk, to supply the church, state and people.

The Silk Road was changing. The Indian traders took the southwest routes via the Karakorum and Kashmir passes into India. The Sogdians continued to trade north through western Turkestan to the Eurasian Steppe. Sericulture had already spread to Merv, and was especially successful around the Caspian Plain. Then a Persian raiding party abducted some Syrian silk weavers and dyers and imprisoned them in their gynaeceum, forcing them to weave silk destined for the Eastern Roman Empire. With the help of the Syrian silk workers, the Persians mastered the art of silk weaving and developed unique patterns and techniques. It was a long time, however, before they could produce sufficient silk for their own use, let alone excess to trade.

Empress Theodora, c500–48 CE the beautiful and capable wife of Justinian, wearing a rich and colourful silk tunic with woven or embroidered border of the Three Magi , a decorated *maniakis* embossed with jewels, and a diadem, called a *stephanos* with cascading pearls and gems. She is accompanied by her most trusted attendant, the eunuch Narsus and her best friend Antoninia, the wife of Justinian's foremost general, Belisarius.

There were intermittent wars between the Persians and Romans and sometimes supplies were cut off altogether. Both the Syrian Desert route and the road to the weaving and dyeing cities of Phoenicia were threatened with bandits and high taxes. Constantinople's ruler Emperor Justinian I (c482–565) actively campaigned to restore the Empire to its ancient limits, reuniting the East and West. He and his stunning wife Theodora (c500–547) were intelligent, ambitious, courageous and very able administrators. She was the daughter of Aracius, a bear-feeder in the amphitheatre at Constantinople and had been what is euphemistically described an actress and dancer. Theodora, as Justinian's powerful and trusted helpmate, frequently bore responsibility for government at home, while he was absent on campaigns. She was generous with her wealth and had a particular interest in the welfare of women, especially those on the streets. Both rulers loved luxury and surrounded themselves with every conceivable extravagance, but were very astute to the needs of both the government and the people. To this day they can be seen in all their finery, in the mosaic frieze in the Church of San Vitale in Ravenna. Theodora always wore the richest silk, splendidly embroidered with stylized flowers and geometric patterns, typical of Byzantium. She stands regally, wearing a white undergown and maniakis embroidered with precious stones and interwoven with gold, and over that a purple palla or mantle embroidered with figures of the Magi. Around her neck she wears a very distinctive gold collar and on her head a heavy diadem with cascades of emeralds and pearls.

With the help of two Nestorian monks, Justinian had established sericulture near Constantinople. Procopius (499–565) his Prefect, was alone in criticizing Theodora, maintaining that she put the whole matter of silk production in the hands of one of her favourites, who created a royal monopoly, secretly enriching himself at the same time. As Theodora died in 547, before the arrival of the monks bringing the knowledge of sericulture, perhaps Procopius was inventing slanderous stories for his own end. Justinian tried to control the production of silk by charging nine chrysos a pound, too expensive for the Persian merchants. It was a time of great unrest and the silk industry collapsed leaving the silk weavers and craftsmen destitute, and many fled to the silk workshops of Persia.

The Islamic religion spread to Turkey, across to North Africa and on to Spain and with it went the silk trade, knowledge of sericulture and weaving the beautiful arabesque brocades. Mohammed was a trader and camel driver and Islam encouraged traders and accorded them high social status. The Byzantine Christians and the Moslems had generally cooperated and traded together, until Pope Urban II, in response to the advance on the Levant by the Saracens, announced the call to the Crusades at the end of the eleventh century. In 1146 Roger II, King of Sicily, conducted raids on Thebes, Athens and Corinth. Greece had its own silk industry, built around the wild tussah varieties of silkworm, not the domesticated Bombyx mori. Nevertheless when Roger II deported silk weavers and embroiderers to Palermo, they were a real prize. The King set the silk workers up in workshops and they helped to establish sericulture and silk weaving and taught the local people. It was another century before sericulture passed from Sicily to Lucca, Venice and Florence in Italy. By 1258 Venice was receiving silk muslins and brocades from Baghdad, Yazd, Malabar and China.

In the late 1300s Samarkand was still a vibrant city, a staging post for vast caravans of over 800 camels bringing fine silks from China and luxury items from the west. People still travelled the Silk Road, the silk traders all year, the Islamic pilgrims mainly during the month of Ramadan. The Moslem world became united by cultural ties and trade, less so politically, and the spread of Islam now effectively cut off Europe from Asia. China under the Ming Dynasty (1366–1644) withdrew and closed its western frontiers, and by the time Constantinople fell in 1453 to the Ottoman Turks, the great days of the Silk Road were over. It is no longer easy to travel the whole length from Ch'ang-an to the Mediterranean. It was virtually abandoned soon after Marco Polo's seventeen years in the Court of Kublai Khan. In remote and ruined desert cities, shards of Chinese pottery and vestiges of ancient silk patterns and designs can still be found, an echo of days long gone.

Polos leaving Venice with its bridges and canals and the Doge Palace on the left. From an English manuscript, c1400, *Les Livres du Graunt Caam*, MS Bodley 264, f218. Bodleian Library, Oxford.

CHAPTER THREE
Marco Polo

Marco Polo's adventure came at a critical time in history. The *'Travels of Marco Polo'* offers an insight into an exciting period of high adventure and exploration on the Old Silk Road. His book was unique in providing a wonderful record of just how extensive silk and sericulture was in thirteenth century Mongol China.

The Saracens were on the march. The Europeans were afraid that the Saracen infidels or unbelievers would conquer and claim the Holy Land and impose their Muslim faith, so on the 27th November 1095, Pope Urban II announced the First Crusade. Christians rallied to the call to join the Holy Army and in the wake of successive Crusades, the route from Europe to the East was opened up. The Italian Mediterranean trading cities of Venice, Genoa and Pisa prospered and expanded. In 1204 Venice attacked and took Constantinople enabling many wealthy Venetian merchants to set up trading posts in the Crimea and around the Black Sea. Venice became the richest and most powerful of the city states and a major sea power. They won both ways; handling and trading goods coming from the East and supplying the army going to the Crusades with transport and provisions. The Venetians were ruthless bargainers and later claimed a half share of all Eastern conquests. The situation was ripe for political and mercantile expansion.

Around the same time, the Tartars of Mongolia, led by the great Genghis Khan (1162–1227) were hell-bent on conquering the whole known world, including the ancient Chinese Empire. When the Khan died, power passed to his third son, Ogadai who reigned until 1241. He was followed by his son Kuyuk and eventually Kublai Khan (1252–1294), a man of great energy, vision and talent, who now controlled most of Central Asia.

The Tartars over-ran the whole of southern Russia, decimated Persia and advanced towards the West, pillaging and subjugating the towns and people as they went. This made many of the rulers of the lands around the Mediterranean extremely anxious. They began to fear the Tartars, the Saracens, and for the survival of the Christian Church. This motivated Pope Alexander IV in 1260 to publish his Papal Bull, *Clamat in auribus* deploring the situation, warning every Christian ruler of the dire state of affairs and calling on the Church and people to respond.

A previous Pope, Innocent IV had tried to defuse the situation and turn the Tartars away from their destructive path, and even better, to convert them to the True Christian Faith. In April 1245 he had sent a very fat, elderly, Italian Franciscan friar, Giovanni di Piano Carpini (c1182–c1253) as an ambassador to Batu Khan. Carpini had very little understanding of the ways of the East, but his 'Voyages', written in 1246, did give a detailed account of Mongol life and laws, costume and society. He recorded the enthronement of Kuyuk, grandson of Genghis Khan and described how Kuyuk stood under a double canopy of silk baldachin cloth while over four thousand ambassadors stood for hours, waiting in the crowd to offer gifts and tribute. These gifts included five hundred carts, full of silver and gold and silken garments, all to be divided later among the Khan's court. Carpini described the rich 'robes of samit and robes of purple and baldachin cloth, silke girdles wrought with gold, costly skines and other gifts'. Baldachin was the name given to a valuable embroidered silk fabric woven from gold and silk. Over the years that changed, and baldachin cloth was more usually a weft faced, shot silk brocade. Carpini and his mission was of minor concern to the Khan and does not seem to have had the slightest effect on him or stopped the advance of his troops on the West.

In 1253 the saintly Louis IX of France sent a French Fleming, Friar William of Rubruk on a religious mission to Karakorum. William was not quite so large or as old as Carpini and had a much greater understanding of the people and their languages. He was the first

European to realize that Cathay was actually China, the home of the silk traders '... from whom are brought the most excellent stuffes of silk'. In his *Journal* he also described the women's garments as being similar to the men's but longer, worn with strange side opening jackets. He was no more effective than Carpini in converting the Khan to Christianity or stopping him advancing on the West.

The Polo Brothers, Nicolo and Matteo

Nicolo and Matteo Polo were therefore not the first Europeans to travel from the West to the Far East. They were merchants, not missionaries. Versions of the story differ, but sometime before 1260, when Marco was still a young child, the Polo brothers left their families in Venice for Constantinople and Soldaia now called Sudak, on the coast of the Crimea to visit their brother Marco senior, a member of the Venetian trading community. The Polos were Venetian merchants, possibly with their own ships, trading in anything that would turn a profit, especially gems. Jewels had high value, were easy to carry, hide and trade. Nicolo and Matteo went on to Sarai, northwest of Astrakhan on the Caspian Sea where Barka Khan welcomed them, accepted their goods, and traded them '... for at least twice their value...' which was most satisfactory.

The Polo brothers stayed twelve months but as the way back was blocked by a bitter local war, they headed eastwards towards the steppes and the Golden Horde, looking to trade in Russia. They crossed the Volga and traveled to Bukhara, where they stayed at the court of Khan Chagatai. Once again the way back was blocked by regional wars and skirmishes so after three years they took the opportunity to accompany an emissary of Kublai Khan to Khanbalik, near modern Beijing.

In 1265 Kublai Khan had been supreme ruler for about five years. He was a hard and powerful man, but among his many endearing qualities was his avid curiosity. He welcomed the Polo brothers warmly and for a year entertained them with feasts, and plied them endlessly with questions about life, religions and customs in the West. He loved miracles, magical signs and portents. If he could be convinced of the superiority of Christianity, then he and all his

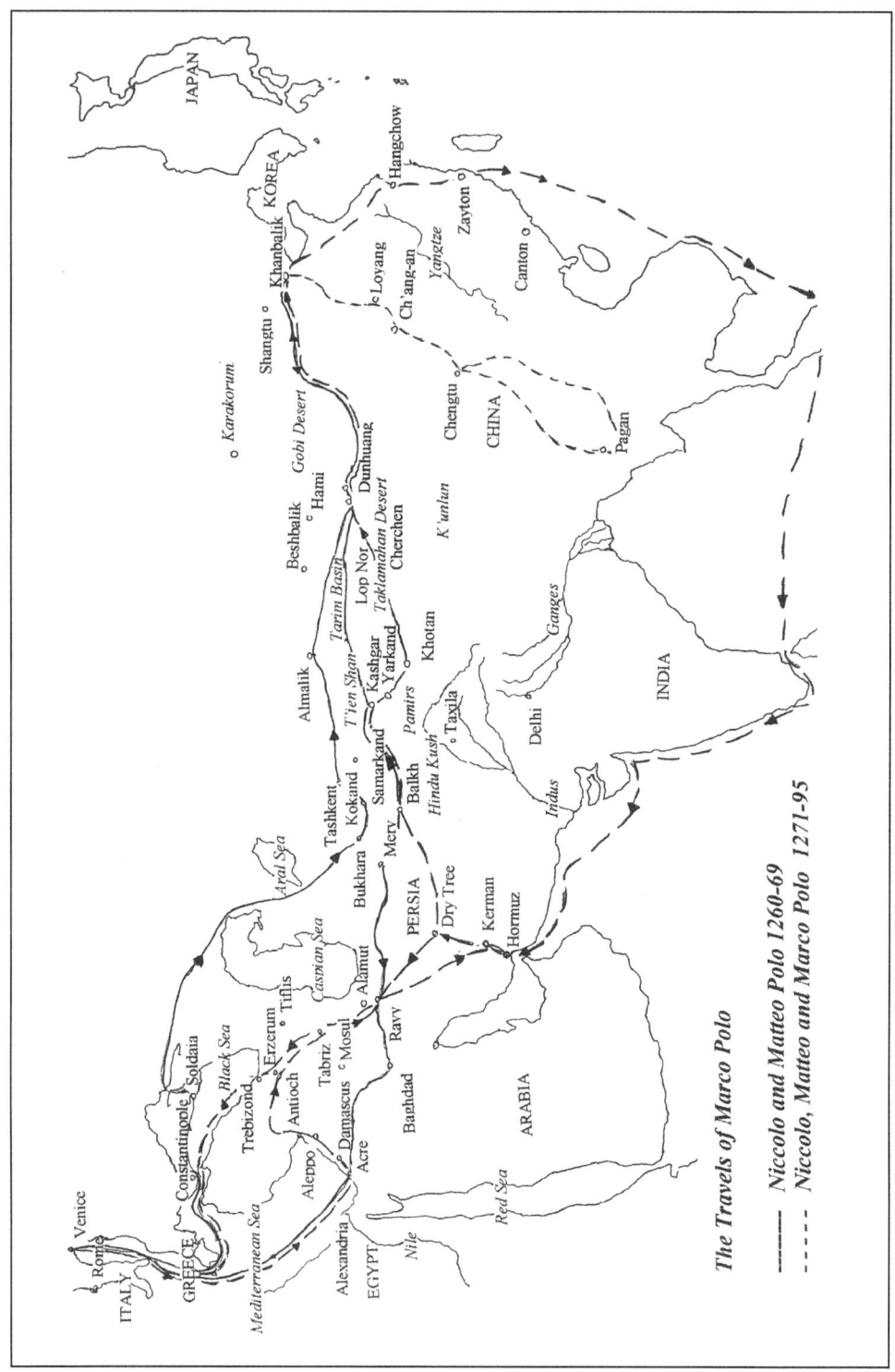

Map of the Travels of Marco Polo, his father and uncle 1260–1295.

court would become Christians.

The Polo brothers took the opportunity to trade and become more fluent in the languages of the Far East, but after a year Kublai Khan reluctantly let them go, on condition that they return to Khanbalik with holy oil from the sepulchre at Jerusalem and one hundred learned doctors of the church. He wanted educated, intelligent men, articulate in theology who could argue the case for Christianity.

The brothers left in the spring of 1266 with the Khan's blessing, supplies for the long journey and a golden tablet to ensure their protection and safe passage. They retraced their route to Bukhara and then straight to the Mediterranean via Baghdad before heading south to Acre, in Palestine, arriving there in April 1269. It had taken over three years to get back because of the appalling conditions, burning deserts, terrible storms, swollen rivers and treacherous, snow covered mountain ranges.

In Acre they told Tebaldo Visconti, (Tebaldo di Piacenza) the Papal Legate for Jerusalem of their travels and the Khan's request. Tebaldo was most interested in the expansion of Christianity, but unfortunately he felt unable to authorize one hundred learned men because that decision would have to come directly from the Pope. The main universities could not supply that many scholarly men at any one time, anyway. Unfortunately there wasn't a Pope either. Pope Clement IV had died in 1268 and, with no news of the election of a new Pope, the brothers decided to return to Venice to see their families and to attend to their businesses.

The Polo brothers had been away from Venice for over ten years, and they were greeted on their return with the sad news that Nicolo's wife had died. The little son Nicolo had left behind had grown into a lively, intelligent and observant young man. Marco was completely enchanted by the tales his father and uncle told of their journey and he was determined not to be left behind again. Possibly he was present in Venice in 1268, and saw the colourful and impressive procession of the guilds before the Palace of St Mark in Venice, to celebrate the institution of the new Doge, Lorenzo Tiepolo. Martino da Canale described the fifty sailing ships and galleys sailing past in the harbour and the guildsmen marching in their ranks, wearing their gorgeous livery. There were furriers appareled in samite and scarlet silk, mantles of ermine and vair and the mercers in silk. The makers of cloth of gold silks of Venice must have left a strong impression on Marco because his book is full of descriptions of wonderful clothes and textiles, especially the silks.

A new Pope had still not been elected. In exasperation the church officials locked the cardinals in conclave to await the puffs of smoke that proclaimed a successful election. In 1271 the three Polos felt they could wait no longer and decided to return to Acre. There they met again with Tebaldo and as there was still no news of a new pope, decided to go and get the holy oil from Jerusalem. They got as far as Laiassus, a rich silk trading port, when a messenger arrived in a great flurry and told them that a new Pope had at last been elected and he was none other than their old friend Tebaldo, now to be known as Pope Gregory X.

The new Pope was still enthusiastic about Christianizing the Mongols but had difficulty in arousing in his clergy a missionary zeal to travel to the far ends of the earth. They had enjoyed a fine lifestyle as part of the Papal Legate's court and were concerned about their careers and most reluctant to exchange the prestige and comfort there for the dangers and discomforts of the unknown road and missionary life. Eventually two Dominicans, Friar Nicolo of Vicenza and Friar William of Tripoli reluctantly accepted the mission to go to the Far East and convert the Mongols and the Chinese. The Pope invested them with wide powers and privileges, but within days the two men had become frightened by the scrapping between the Egyptians and the Armenians and fearful for their lives. They thrust the Papal Papers and Privileges into the Polos' hands, and scurried back to Acre, and the security of the Papal court. With a heavy heart, the Polos decided to travel on, at all speed. They were very concerned that the Khan would not take kindly to both the delay and the lack of men to argue the case for Christianity.

The Journey

Marco loved travelling and was obviously delighted with all he saw, especially the silks. He was very observant, but as a traveller and

Messer Marco Polo, a fashionable young man. From the first German edition of his Travels, printed in Nuremberg in 1477.

merchant, he tended to declare that all silks were the finest and richest, rather than note the differences. Nevertheless, the book of his travels offers a unique picture of the breadth of sericulture and the beautiful silks produced in Mongol China at the time.

Marco made notes as they travelled. When they passed through Turkey, he saw that the Greeks and Armenians made a livelihood from trade and crafts and he declared that the carpets of dyed crimson silks and other rich and delicate colours were the finest of all. They travelled on to Turkomania past Mt Ararat and Marco mentioned the oil field of Baku, on the inland Caspian Sea. He found evidence of Genoese traders who crossed the mountainous area of Ghelan and brought back the silk known by the same name. He was amazed by the abundance of 'silken fabrics and cloth of gold . . . the finest ever seen', woven in Tiflis. He was interested in the different religions and races of men, Arabs who worshiped Mohammed, Nestorians, Jacobites and Christians. The Georgians he noted, were Orthodox Christians and depended on trade for their livelihood. He mentioned the beautiful silk fabrics and cloth of gold, woven in the capital Tbilisi, and compared the silk and gold fabric called nasich, or nakh with the brocades, damask and cramoisy or crimson cloth, richly decorated with beasts and birds, made in Baldach. (Baghdad).

The Polos continued their journey to Erzurum and Tabriz. It was a great commercial city with quantities of valuable cloth of gold brought there from India, Baghdad and Mosul, including the material known as mosulin. At that time, it was woven from silk and gold thread and only later was made from cotton. Marco was less impressed by the large number of Latins and other traders he met there, who he thought were particularly wicked and treacherous.

In Baldach he described the manufacture of silk wrought with gold, and in particular the damasks and velvets ornamented with figures of birds and beasts. This 'velluti' was probably carpet rather than velvet cloth. He found silk and gold cloth traded at Tauris in Iraq and in Yazd, and a woven silk of the same name. It was in great demand by the merchants who made a good profit exporting it all over the known world. The Polos were heading for the city state of Kerman, via Saveh where the tomb of the Three Magi, Gaspar, Melchior and

The Polos at Hormuz on the Persian Gulf. The ships they were offered were overloaded, in this illustration with an elephant, horse and camel, and very unseaworthy. From *Le Livre des Merveilles du Monde*.
By permission of the Bibliotheque Nationale, Paris.

Balthazar was believed to be located. After that, it was seven more hard days riding over the salt plains. It was an extremely unpleasant part of the journey in the intense heat. They were attacked by some bandits, the Karaunas, on the Kerman uplands and were lucky to escape with their lives. Once in Kerman they could relax and Marco was happy to watch the pretty girls there, embroidering birds and animals and other designs in multi-coloured silks on to curtains and bedcovers.

They continued their travels south for another two hundred miles to the Gulf of Hormuz, in the hope of getting a boat and making up for lost time, but the boats they were offered were flimsy and ramshackle, rough boards stitched together with loose twine and coconut husk and caulked with an extremely smelly fish glue. They feared that the small craft was altogether too risky to take on the open sea, so after much discussion they reluctantly retraced their steps back across the plains of Rudbar to Kerman. There was one hundred miles of desert to cross, with practically no water, huge gravel slopes and sand hills, occasional salt lakes, and sun-bleached animal skeletons. Eventually they reached temperate Tabas and the crossroads of Kerman. There was no further trouble from the Karaunas but the green brackish water from the Persian sulphur springs made them very ill. For another eight days they travelled across the arid land to Tun, in northern Persia, to the old landmark of the Solitary or Dry Tree, believed to have marked the final battle between Darius of Persia and Alexander the Great.

Assassin Country

The Polos now passed into the territory Marco calls Mulehet, the land of the Assassins. A powerful, sinister man called Sheikh Alaodin, known as the Old Man of the Mountain had reigned amid splendor in a fortified castle at Alamut south of the Caspian Sea. Although the sect had been destroyed by Hulegu Khan's army sixteen years before Marco travelled through the region, the threat of violence was still very real. Sheikh Alaodin had headed a heretical Ismaili Moslem sect, founded originally at the end of the eleventh century. He ruled through convincing the simple mountain people that he was a prophet, the Vice-regent of God. He gathered around him fearless, audacious boys aged between twelve and twenty and gave them hashish, and while in a drugged sleep, took them into a secret garden, full of all kinds of earthly delights, wine, music and beautiful girls. The boys woke up believing that they were in Paradise and agreed to do anything the Old Man ordered, just to be allowed to stay. He trained them in the language, rites, and rituals of the marked men, then sent them off on missions of assassination, hence the corruption of hashashin to assassins. The boys were quite willing to do the will of the Old Man, believing that whether they lived or died, they would be in Paradise. There were hundreds of calculated murders, including two leading Crusader lords in the Holy Land, Conrad the King of Jerusalem and Raymond, Count of Tripoli.

The three Polos rested for a considerable period in Badakhshan while Marco recovered from a severe illness. They headed for Bukhara and Samarkand, through the mountain ranges of the Hindu Kush and the High Pamirs, known as the Roof of the World. It was hard going but they felt the benefit of the clean mountain air, and Marco delighted in the flowering trees and trout streams. It became bitterly cold, and they had difficulty cooking in the thin air at such a high

Sheik Alodin, known as the Old Man of the Mountains, in the Garden of Paradise, Assassin country, where delights were offered to young men and boys in exchange for becoming killers.
From *Le Livre du Graunt Caam*, MS Bodley 264, fol. 226 Bodleian Library, Oxford.

altitude. It still required forty days of extremely arduous travel over the desolate country of Beloro with plateaus between 13,000 and 15,000 feet, and peaks 19,000 feet above sea level. They saw the wild curly-horned mountain sheep, later named *Ovis poli* after Marco Polo. They then chose the direct but more difficult route round the southern side of the Taklimakan desert via Kashgar, Khotan, and Pem where there was jasper and jade and the local custom of a woman welcoming a stranger if her husband had been away for more than twenty days.

It took the Polos five exhausting days to trek across the salt flats to the town of Lop Nor, near the edge of the Great Gobi desert. Silk was part of the cremation rituals there, and the houses of mourning were hung with silk and cloth of gold. The Polos needed to take food for another month for both men and beasts to cross the desert to Dunhuang. Marco writes of hallucinations, heat haze, phantom desert sounds of wailing, drum beats, spirit voices, and attacking robbers. There was also the danger of falling asleep and going round in circles. At night they had to put up a flag before they went to sleep so they would set out in the right direction in the morning through the formless landscape.

Finally they reached the Caves of the Thousand Buddha's, at Dunhuang which Marco described as 'abbeys and monasteries full of all kinds of idols, to which they (the inhabitants) offer great sacrifices, and pay great honour and worship.' In the nineteenth century, the explorer-missionaries Francesca French and Mildred Cable called it the 'art gallery of the desert'.

The Caves at Dunhuang

The Mogao Caves are twenty-five kilometres southeast of Dunhuang. Around 366CE the monk Lo-tsun had a vision of rays of light, shining like a thousand Buddha's in a cloud of glory. The monk encouraged a rich and pious pilgrim to have a cave painted by a local artist, and then dedicated to the Buddha as a shrine and to his own safe return. Other travellers, already exhausted and frightened by the dangers of travel across the arid deserts, sought protection by following suit. Before long there were about a thousand decorated caves, although only four hundred and sixty nine now remain. It became a centre for worship, with temples and valuable artifacts.

Around 1000 CE some of the treasures were walled up in a secret cave, probably to save the sacred Buddhist texts from falling into the hands of the barbarians. In 1907 the explorer Marc Aurel Stein bribed the caretaker, Abbot Wang Yuan-lu into opening the hidden cave, known as Cave Number 17. Inside was a priceless hoard of over 50,000 manuscripts, written in many different languages, including Sanskrit, Chinese, Sogdian, Tibetan, and Uighur. As well, there were exquisite embroideries and carved figures, all dated to between 400 and 900CE. It was the find of the century, a treasure trove.

Abbot Wang, the custodian at the Caves of a Thousand Buddhas. Marc Aurel Stein persuaded him to open up Cave 17, a treasure trove.

Old Caves of a Thousand Buddhas at Mogao 25 kms from Dunhuang as rediscovered by Marc Aurel Stein in 1908.

Some of the three hundred Buddhist paintings were obviously temple banners with broad floating streamers on the sides, so long they could have hung from the cliff tops above the caves. Many had a single sacred figure or Bodhisattva, Buddha himself, Lokapala or 'Guardian of the World" depicted on them. The votive hangings were painted on incredibly fine silk gauze, silk brocade or paper, mounted on a backing of cloth or paper and carefully patched and darned. Other sacred hangings feature a group of divine figures or scenes from the Buddhist heaven. Aurel Stein had twenty-four cases of manuscripts and five of paintings and embroideries and similar art relics, packed and sent back to the British Museum. The silk scrolls and banners, long squashed under bundles of manuscripts had become compressed, almost impossible to open. It took British Museum staff years to meticulously unfold them and reveal their secrets.

The Polos continued their journey. Marco was interested in everything he saw, including asbestos at Chinchitalas near Kara Khoja. It was found as a vein in the mountain, and the woolly fibres were dried, pounded, washed and finally spun and woven under the strict control of the Khan's officers. Marco was amazed that it was cleaned by just throwing it in the fire. He mentioned also the 'stones that burn like logs' although coal was known in Europe at the time. He was impressed by the first and second class Imperial Postal Service, and the facility for top priority dispatches, not seen in Europe since the fall of the Roman Empire. He approved of the number of baths taken daily and the oriental obsession with cleanliness. He observed the wide use of paper money and the concept of credit.

Several times each year the merchants arrived with their caravans stuffed with silks and other precious commodities. The items were examined and a value assigned to them and then exchanged for paper money. The Khan's mint manufactured the paper money from the bark of the mulberry trees. The black fibrous inner layer was removed and glue added to the pounded bark before it was rolled out into a kind of paper. It was then cut into squares and rectangles equivalent to half a Venetian silver groat, bigger ones were worth a groat, and others equaled five and ten groats, up to one, two and ten bezants. Special officials wrote their names on the notes and authenticated them by stamping them with the Great Khan's seal sprinkled with vermilion pigment. There were severe punishments for anyone found forging the paper money. Marco thought this was how the Khan had become so unimaginably rich, he could just make money. He was less aware that the treasury had to be backed up by real silver and gold.

Kublai Khan and his Household

After crossing the deserts the Polos finally arrived in May 1275 to a warm welcome and the comforts of the Khan's great summer hunting palace at Shang-tu, immortalized by the poet Samuel Taylor Coleridge as Xanadu. Marco was impressed by this temporary palace, cleverly made with spliced cane struts, silken guy-ropes, weatherproofed felt and lined with furs and costly silks. It was a

Kublai Khan 1215–94, grandson of Genghis Khan and powerful leader and founder of the Yuan Dynasty in China.

palace inside the royal estate, and included sixteen miles of enclosed parkland, stocked with deer, gyrfalcons and other game, even a tame cheetah. Everything was luxurious, exceeding anything they had seen in the West. The walls of his main palace at Khanbalik were also covered with gold and silver, decorated with pictures of dragons, birds and horsemen. There were exquisite textiles and beautiful silk carpets of many colours and the main hall was so vast, six thousand men could eat there.

Marco became completely overwhelmed by the numbers. The Khan had an enormous entourage of over ten thousand people to be accommodated. He had four Empresses each with their own courts of three hundred ladies in waiting, and twenty-two sons by these wives. As well, there were his carefully chosen concubines, giving him another twenty-five sons, styled Baron and also groomed for government. There were pages, servants and eunuchs, actors, musicians, court officials and physicians along with two hundred or more new concubines added every other year from the Province of Ungut. In addition there were 25,000 prostitutes to service the visiting ambassadors and all had to be appropriately clothed. It required unlimited amounts of silk and other beautiful fabrics and the court tailors and seamstresses were kept extremely busy.

In addition, there was the Khan's private guard of twelve thousand Barons who needed embroidered gowns, one for each of the thirteen solemn feast days of the lunar year, a total of 156,000 garments, replaced every ten years. The Great Khan's thirteen special Lunar Festival outfits were made of even richer material and emblazoned with even finer jewels. For the New Year celebrations in February everyone wore white, considered a lucky colour. People brought the Khan costly gifts of gold, silver, precious jewels, pearls, white horses and lengths of white silk. Even his five thousand elephants walking in procession, had tented housings on their backs covered with birds and beasts embroidered in silk. The Khan was born on the 28th September 1214 so for his birthday celebrations each year, he wore his best robe of silk cloth of gold with a priceless gold belt. The twelve hundred members of his council wore similar garments of gold coloured silk with fine leather boots and a girdle of chamois leather, all embroidered with gold and silver thread. Some garments were worth up to one thousand bezants each.

Marco Polo 1254–1324 wearing Tartar hunting garments.

The city of Khanbalik was one of the greatest mercantile cities in the eastern world. At least one thousand cartloads of raw silk, gold tissue and silks of various kinds were sent there every day, and traders came to buy and sell. The rich were dressed in sumptuous, valuable clothes of silk and gold with precious furs of ermine, sable, squirrel and fox. The poor did not wear silk, but were tithed one tenth or worked one day a week to process silk, wool or hemp and this woven cloth was stored or distributed as gifts to dependents or envoys or as clothing for the troops.

The Khan noted Marco's intelligence, discretion and ability with languages and over the years he sent him to most parts of the Mongol Empire, including many of the thriving centres of sericulture and the silk trade. Marco came back with a full account of the business, and lots of interesting snippets, occurrences, stories and anecdotes which delighted the Khan. Marco learnt to speak Mongol, Turkish and Persian and had a smattering of Chinese but could not read it.

Marco's first mission for the Khan took over 4 months. First he went to Gouza where gold tissue was manufactured, and on to Cho-chau which produced cloths of silk and gold and a thin rich silk called sendal. Ten days ride from Cho-chau he visited the Kingdom of Tái-Yuan-Fu and noted the many mulberry trees and the vast amount of silk produced there. A further seven days journey west took him to the city of Píng-yang-fu, which was crowded with merchants. There the people lived by trading the silk they produced. There was also a thriving silk industry and commerce in silk around Cuncun where the ginger and silk products were ferried down the Yellow River. Two days further to Ka-chan-fu (Cachanfu), there was another silk manufacturing centre with many artisan's shops and factories producing silken cloth and gold tissue of every kind. Within three days journeying, there were many more cities and towns including Ken-zan-fu, all engaged in the silk industry.

At Vochan he noted the custom of tattooing the body, of gold fillings in the teeth and of the father taking his new-born baby to bed for forty days, because the mother had already cared for it for the last nine months, a practice known as couvade. All the business and trade was done by the women, the men were the hunters. He found that silver was worth five times more than gold, and the merchants used a tally stick with notches on both sides, similar to tally sticks used in England at the time. It was split down the middle and both parties each kept half, as a record and proof. There were some omissions from his account; no mention of the Great Wall, women's bound feet, never accepted by Mongol women, cormorants fishing or tea drinking although he visited tea growing areas. Perhaps he had grown accustomed to these things, and just took them for granted.

Marco was by now the eyes and ears of the Khan and he made careful notes as he travelled. The cities of Chin-ti-gui and Chang-li manufactured silk and exported it down the river. Pazan-fu had abundant silk, including woven tissues of gold and very fine scarves. After six days of travelling, he arrived at Tudin-fu, which had been a major centre for the collection and trade of large quantities of beautiful silks before the city was subjugated by the Khan. Marco then went to the province of Shantung, which he called Manji. In the town of Pau-ghin there was a great deal of silk and woven gold tissue, as there was in Nan-ghin and Sa-yan-fu. Chan-ghian-fu, he said produced the finest quality raw silk mixed with gold. Four days later he arrived at Tin-gui-gui, a city famous for its raw silk. He was impressed by the many rich merchants who lived in the magnificent city of Sin-gui and enormous quantities of silk manufactured there, not only for domestic consumption but also for other markets. He went on to Kue-lin-fu where the beautiful women wore luxurious silk garments, made in the district. The city of Ungen exported much of the silk produced locally in this rich silk growing region. Finally he went to Pagan, before returning to Khanbalik by a roundabout route.

Marco went on many trips for the Khan. He obviously loved the fabulous city of Kinsai now Hangchow, the intellectual centre of old China in the Sung period. It was the repository of literature, poetry, essays and printed books, two hundred years before Europe discovered movable type. Marco noticed everything, including the luxurious silk clothes produced there and worn by the inhabitants. Even the carriages and barges on the river were lined with silk. He noted the funeral custom of throwing silk, wrought with gold onto the burning pyre. He went south to Kara-jang in Yunnan province near Burma, which he called 'Tibet,' where elephants were used in battle. He then goes on to describe the camel hair, silk and gold woven in Tibet, and the trade in sendal and other silks and cloth of gold at Ho-Kien-Fu.

Return to Venice

After seventeen years in China, the Polo's longed to see Venice again but doubted if the Khan, now in his seventies, would ever let them go home. They had been very privileged but they could not be sure of their continued protection under a new ruler. In 1290 Marco returned from India, and the Polo's saw their chance to offer to escort Princess Kokachin, a daughter of the royal household and the new bride for Arghun, the Ilkan of Persia. The Khan reluctantly let them go but with good grace. He fitted out their party lavishly, gave them letters and gifts for the Pope and passports stamped with gold.

In 1292 Marco was still only 38, but by now Nicolo and Matteo were elderly men. The three Polos and the wedding party, including three envoys and a large group of attendants, set off from the busy port of Zaitun in fourteen great Chinese junks, five of which were large enough to require crews of 260 men. It took twenty-one months to sail to the Persian Gulf, only to find that Arghun Khan had died and his brother Kaikhatu had usurped the throne. The Polo's had grown very fond of the Princess and were concerned about her safety and happiness, so after discussion with her she was given in marriage to Arghun's son, Prince Ghazan. He was at the time patrolling the marshes, near the region of the Solitary or Dry Tree in the province of Timochain. Ghazan seems to have been short and stocky and a fierce warrior, but very kind, and he loved Kokachin dearly. The Polos stayed a further nine months and it was during this time in 1294 that they received the sad news that Kublai Khan had died, at the advanced age of eighty years. Things turned out well for Ghazan, with a happy marriage and eventually, rightful accession to his throne.

Rather than heading for the Mediterranean, the Polos travelled north to the port of Trebizond on the Black Sea and took a ship, arriving in Venice in 1295. After twenty-three years, they were not recognized and were turned away as tramps so they decided to give a great banquet and invite all their family and old friends. At each course they put on another layer of their Tartar finery, ending with

Princess Kokachin, hand-painted Persian miniature of the little princess that the Polo's accompanied on the long journey across China to be the bride of Arghun, the Ilkan of Persia.

Marco Polo 61

Marco Polo dictating his story to Rusticello of Pisa, as reprinted in Henry Yule's 1874 edition of *The Book of Ser Marco Polo*.

the rough travelling clothes. Finally, with a flourish, they ripped them open at the seams and out tumbled the gorgeous gems sewn secretly within the lining.

The story does not end there for in 1298 Marco was made a 'gentleman commander' on a galley, involved in yet another skirmish between Genoa and Venice. He was captured and put in goal and it was in Genoa that he shared a cell with a scribe, Rusticello of Pisa who was so enthralled by his adventures that Marco sent to Venice for his notes and diaries and Rusticello wrote the stories down as Marco related them. Marco was released after a treaty was signed in May 1299 and *'The Travels of Marco Polo'* appeared not long after and was a resounding success. Marco married Donata and had three daughters, Fantina, Bellela and Moreta. After the deaths of his father and uncle, he continued to trade on his own account and his name appeared in various court records. In 1305 he was mentioned as *'Nobilis Marcus Polo Milioni'* standing surety for a wine smuggler. In 1311 he sued a dishonest agent who owed him money on a sale of musk, and in 1323 he was in dispute over a party wall. While he led an interesting life after his return to Venice, judging by his nickname, il Milioni which he acquired from his constant retelling of his fantastic tales, it would seem that his life was now but a pale shadow of his years at the court of the Great Kublai Khan. He died around twenty-five years later in 1324 aged seventy years and left his fortune to

Camels waiting at dawn near the Crescent Lake and Singing Sands at Mogao, 25kms from Dunhuang.

his daughters. On his deathbed, Marco maintained that he had told not one half of what he had really seen. He did in fact include many tall stories, but also much is surprisingly accurate, and later travellers like Marc Aurel Stein and Sven Hedin have discovered places that accurately match his description.

The Various Versions of Marco Polo's Travels

There are eighty-five manuscript copies of the 'Travels', written in Latin, Italian and French and seventy-five editions in twelve languages, all vary. None of Rusticello's original manuscripts still exist and none of the extant versions are complete. Rusticello wrote in French, though Ramusio, one of the translators says he wrote in Latin. Rumusio's Italian edition (R) contains the fullest account. A Paris MS (F) is considered to be nearest the original. (L) is a Latin compendium and (V) is a corrupt version in the Venetian dialect. Ronald Latham's *The Travels of Marco Polo* was based on Professor Benedetto's Latin edition of (Z). An Italian edition by Daniele Ponchireli with a preface by Sergio Solmi (Torino 1954) is based on a Paris manuscript. There are many other variations, versions, translations and editions including Bartoli, (Firenze 1863) and Alluli (Milano 1928). Sir Henry Yule's translation and revision of 1871 has been used extensively by other scholars and is valuable for its notes.

Doubting Thomas, one of the scenes from the Syon cope 1300-20. The air of pathos, large expressive black rimmed eyes, stripy hair and great attention to muscular construction render these embroideries truly *acupictura*, like painting with a needle.

With permission of the Victoria & Albert Museum, London.

CHAPTER FOUR
English Medieval Embroidery

The Golden Age of English Embroidery: what a magic picture that paints of medieval women sitting at their embroidery making the most exquisite items for themselves and the church. The spread of Christianity to Britain early in the sixth century and improved communications with Rome, where supplies of silk were available, had heightened the desire to import silk to embellish the Church and court. Silk was always expensive, so embroidery was a way to enhance plain silk fabric and add even more value. The possession of these beautiful items was seen as an outward and visible sign of wealth, distinction and power.

Silk was always imported into England, because sericulture was never successfully established there. Silk arrived as small bolts or lengths of woven fabric to sew or embroider, or as raw silk to be spun into thread for embroidery, braid weaving or net making. The Middle Ages was an intensely Christian era and so a pictorial style of embroidery developed, based on the Holy Family and the lives of the saints, birds, flowers and animals, designs similar to those depicted in illuminated manuscripts and stained glass windows. The fine split stitches were minute and the use of subtly dyed silk floss enabled the embroideries to exhibit great sensitivity and tenderness. Fine stitches, underside couching, brick and satin stitch often completely covered the ground of the fabric, and designs could be enhanced with additional goldwork and gems. This time-consuming embroidery, using the finest silk and mostly in the service of the Church came to be known as English Work, *Opus Anglicanum*.

Silk was a luxury item and because of its cost and scarcity was the preserve of wealthy, leisured noble women. Spinning silk and doing embroidery were womanly accomplishments, symbolic of their status, an added refinement; not to earn their living but to enhance their reputation as the elegant lady of the manor or as a desirable marriage prospect. It was usual for noble parents to place their daughters in the household of their feudal lord or sovereign to be educated and trained in the feminine arts necessary for their status in life. Walter de Biblesworth described a charming scene in 1300, of the little heiress Diane de Montchesney being tidied and coiffed after supper and taught to embroider with silk, under the direction of her tutoress.

Owning and being able to embroider silk had great prestige, as valuable as owning land. Bede describes how the first Abbot of Wearmouth made his fifth trip to Rome in 685 CE and brought back with him two large exotic silk scarves or palls. The sale of these exquisite items must have realized a vast sum because it was sufficient to enable him to purchase the land of three families at the mouth of the River Wear, for the site of his new monastic community. An Anglo-Saxon sheriff of Buckingham was prepared to grant a woman called Alwid two hides of land, provided she taught his daughter to embroider. The ability to do refined embroidery was a necessary skill if your daughter was to marry well and you and your family were to go up in the world. Denbart, when he was the Bishop of Durham, granted for life the income of a farm of two hundred acres to an embroideress called Eanswitha, in exchange for repairing and maintaining the clergy's vestments. The 1086 Doomsday survey of land holdings has references to skilled embroiderers, including Leofgyd and Aelfgyd. Leofgyd was a *servientes regis*, a lowly English widow, yet she had stature and some importance because she held three and a half hides of land at Knook and did gold embroidery for the King and Queen.

Silk and embroidery are sometimes mentioned in early records although very few actual examples remain. One of the earliest finds, dated during the Roman occupation of Britain around 250 CE, is a

A woman of around 1280, depicted as Eve spinning. She wears a linen hat with a wimple under the chin, pinned up on top of her head and covered with a net. Her kirtle was loose fitting, with added braid at the hem.
Sketch taken from Add. 38116 ff 8b 13.

fragment of silk twill from a child's grave at Holeborough in Kent, while another came from a fourth century grave at Colchester. This was a dull, rough piece of woven 'grege' silk with the gum still in it, probably originally from China. A seventh century child's relic box at Updown cemetery also contained silk threads. There is something gentle, protective and cherishing about silk, so when a child died, tucking a tiny precious fragment into the little coffin was one of the last loving things a grieving parent could do.

Embroidering silk was considered an honourable task for pious noble women. St Etheldreda, who died in 679, made an exquisite stole and maniple, embroidered with gold and precious stones, while she was Abbess of Ely, which she offered to St Cuthbert (c 635–87), Prior of Lindisfarne. They might be similar to another set which Queen Aelfflaed, wife of King Edward the Elder, commissioned between 909 and 916 for the use of Bishop Frithstan of Winchester. This set was also gifted to St Cuthbert's tomb and parts are still extant and preserved at Durham Cathedral. These treasured items are worked in gold and coloured silk floss on silk fabric and feature prophets, clergy and saints including St John the Baptist and Peter the Deacon, with birds, lions and acanthus sprays. Another Queen, Aelgifu, the second wife of Canute, designed and embroidered ecclesiastical vestments and church furnishings which Canute later presented to the Abbeys of Croyland and Romsey. Queen Edgitha (Edith), wife of Edward the Confessor (1042–66) is said to have been a dutiful wife and embroidered the rich robes that he wore at major festivals. She was skilled in *'d'or et argent brudure,'* and her skill at doing this exquisite gold and silver embroidery led William of Malmesbury to describe her as the 'perfect mistress of her needle'.

The hagiographers who wrote the lives of saints and other important people delighted in reporting a noble lady's dedication and skill. It reinforced their belief in appropriate behaviour for a royal lady, offering the work of her hands to the glory of God and the Church. One writer waxed lyrical in describing how Queen Margaret of Scotland (1045–99) had '. . . a chamber that was like the workshop of a heavenly artist, copes for singers, chasubles, stoles, altar cloths, and other priestly vestments. Church ornaments were always to be seen, some in the course of preparation, others worthy of admiration, already completed'.

Monasticism and Embroidery

The years between 1000 and 1200 were known as the high period of monasticism, when many profoundly spiritual men and women were attracted to a life of prayer and devotion within the confines of a monastery or nunnery. Thomas of Ely records that Queen Aelgiva's daughter, the Lady Aethelswitha, refused marriage and chose to enter a nunnery near Coveney. There she devoted herself to gold embroidery, which she later presented to Ely Cathedral. Thomas says she worked the silk 'with her own hands', which suggests that she actively sewed the fabric and not just directed her maids. There is no suggestion that a noble woman had to give up her maids when she espoused a life of poverty, chastity and humility. The priority was to be free of earthly demands to give oneself fully to God and prayer.

Beautiful textiles were highly valued and gratefully received, and were an opportunity for enclosed and pious nuns like Aethelswitha and Christina of Markyate (c1123) to dedicate the work of their hands to God. Christina was a fine needlewoman and while Prioress,

Holy Family, with the Virgin Mary embroidering, Spain 15thc.

embroidered many beautiful things, including three mitres and a pair of 'sandals', which were probably soft indoor shoes. Abbot Robert de Goreham (1151–66) offered them to Pope Adrian IV (1154–9), and they were so beautiful that the Pope accepted them.

The cloister was one of the few options available to an aristocratic woman who did not wish to, or could not marry. It required a more modest dowry than marriage, so the nunneries accepted not only daughters who desperately desired to live a life devoted to God, but also unwanted daughters, illicit daughters of priests and plain, afflicted or handicapped well-born girls. The nunneries also took in children to be educated, widows who refused to marry again and troublesome eminent women prisoners who had been told by the court to 'get thee to a nunnery'. Many women saw life in a convent as a pleasant and safe place to live, away from a demanding or violent husband and endless pregnancies. Some widowed queens chose to endow a convent, while other distinguished women seized the opportunity to realize their own ambitions and become powerful leaders of communities and controllers of their time and wealth.

Life in a convent could be very demanding if it was an enclosed order, strictly supervised and devoted to prayer and good works. For women in the less strict convents, it could be exceedingly pleasant, with little jaunts on pilgrimages or visits to their family, gossip and chatter over a glass or more of wine in the evening. There were various amusements: minstrels, dancing, embroidering costumes and preparing for the Passion Plays, mumming and enthusiastic feasting on holy days. Some women kept pets, a cow, monkeys, squirrels, rabbits, larks, and at Nevers, there was a parrot called Vert-Vert. Lady Audley, a widow who boarded at the convent of Langley, had to be chastised and stopped from taking all twelve of her little dogs into chapel, because they made such a noise and a fuss that no-one could concentrate on the psalms.

By the late fourteenth century, conditions in some small nunneries had become very lax. Some bishops saw supervising the nunneries as a real bother. Bishop Alnwick dutifully made the rounds of the nunneries in his diocese and took each member aside to ask them searching questions about the running of the establishment. Out it all poured, the late nights, the men who visited, the wandering off, the children born to the nuns, the misuse of funds and the time spent on embroidery.

The bishops were constantly irritated by the way the women, especially the widows, paraded in their beautiful silk gowns, open at the sides and trimmed with fur. The women flaunted their silk and gold girdles and trailed their long silk veils, worn in defiance of the Rule under which they were supposed to live in a state of modesty and humility. But it had become the custom to give the nuns a dress allowance rather than provide them with clothes in common, and so they took advantage of the lenient conditions. Who could blame them for wanting to wear the fashionable and delightful clothes sent to them, or their desire to embroider something precious to give to a friend or relative. Some fashionable women in the community even shaved the hair on their temples and tucked the rest under an exotic embroidered headdress and exposed their high foreheads. It just would not do, and the bishops fumed and ranted, but to no avail. The women always managed to find ways to sweeten a life of restriction and ennui. Time was of no moment, days flowed into months. Their families could afford to send them lengths of silk and bundles of brightly coloured silk floss and they could embroider.

Even the question of what they should embroider caused a problem, because some bishops viewed silk work with suspicion and were critical of the time spent on the fine work. They felt it all took up far too much time that should be devoted to prayer and good works, reading or singing hymns. They maintained that the women should be mending the clothes of the poor, not sewing blood-bands and little caps and bags for friends. Embroidery could only be accepted in the nunneries if it did not interfere with or distract the women from following the Rule. Some Abbesses thought the women should be doing embroidery, because idleness left an opportunity for the devil to come and make mischief.

Although many of the women in the convents had sufficient skills and certainly did embroidery, it is unlikely that all but the largest nunneries under the patronage of the wealthiest families could afford to accept large commissions. Most nunneries were small and often poverty-stricken, especially in the later Middle Ages. The exquisite vestments and church furnishings would have required a heavy financial outlay in silk, gold and gems, as well as secure storage. Many nunneries did have extensive collections of beautiful embroideries, probably made by the enclosed women. The 1485 Records of the Benedictine monastery of Langley mentions a whole sacristy full of embroideries, including altar frontals and vestments. One was black damask, embroidered with roses and stars, and another was white, embroidered with 'rede trewlyps'. They were actually 'true lover's knots', not Turkish tulips which were still unknown in England at the time.

But there was another problem. The women's embroidery was so exquisite that it became a very desirable gift for a bishop to give, perhaps even to the Pope, so time spent on embroidery was tolerated. It is not really possible to tell if the Clare chasuble, made of dark blue silk twill before 1294 and probably commissioned by Margaret de Clare, sometime wife of Edmund Plantagenet, nephew of King Henry III, was the work of a nunnery or professional embroiderers. The copes given by Lanfranc, Archbishop of Canterbury (1070–89), heavy with gold thread and embroidered with dragons and strange birds, were probably made by male embroiderers within Christ Church or by secular male professionals. It was usually only the men's names that were registered as designers, agents, patrons or embroiderers; women's work was almost always unrecorded. The only known piece of *Opus Anglicanum*, apparently done by a woman in a nunnery, is an altar frontal, dated 1290–1340, with the words **DOMNA IOHANNA BEVER LAI MONACA ME FECIT** embroidered in black on the back. The black silk has now mostly decayed, the dye having rotted the silk.

Commissioned Embroidery

The Church seemed to have no objection to the use of non-religious symbols or the conversion of secular garments. In her will written in 1083, the year she died, Matilda, Queen of William the Conqueror, wrote:

> *'I give to the Abbey of the Holy Trinity (at Caen, which she had founded) my tunic worked at Winchester by Aeldret's wife and the mantle embroidered with gold, which is in my chamber,*

Clare Chasuble, 1272–94. The silver-gilt threads are worked on the dark blue silk twill ground, with the central panel containing scenes of the Crucifixion, Virgin and Child, Peter and Paul and the Stoning of Stephen.
With permission of the V&A Museum, London.

to make a cope. Of my two golden girdles, I give that which is ornamented with emblems for the purpose of suspending the lamp before the great altar.'

The 1295 inventory of St Paul's included two copes embroidered with the startling depiction of knights fighting. The 1368 Norfolk inventory notes vestments embroidered with castles, gold crowns, silver and gold stars, flowers, mythical birds and beasts, along with the donor's monogram or coat of arms. In 1491 Sir Gervase Clifton instructed that 'all the altar cloths of silk, a bed of gold Bawdkyne and another bed of russet satin which belonged to . . . (Archbishop Boothe of York) be delivered to make vestments' for use in various chantries in Southwell Minster.

Peter the Deacon, part of the set of stole and maniple given at the instigation of Queen Aelfflaed to St Cuthbert's shrine. Worked in Winchester on a silk ground in surface couching using pure gold wrapped around a silk core, split and stem stitches (909–918). By permission of the Dean and Chapter Durham Cathedral.

The value of fine English embroidery depended on the complexity of the design, finesse of its execution and quality of the metal thread, gems and silk. Hand spinning gold thread and wrapping it around a core of yellow silk was a skilled occupation requiring a seven-year apprenticeship. Poor quality gold tarnished and so its quality was highly regulated by the Guilds. Top quality Cyprus gold thread was used in the tenth century stole and maniple from St Cuthbert's tomb. The main embroidery stitch was underside couching, which attached the gold thread to the surface, forming a little hinge on the wrong side. In later years a less effective but faster method of surface couching was used. Much of the gold thread was actually silver-gilt and was combined with pearls and other gems, making the embroidered item immensely valuable and often very heavy too. Master silk embroiderers or 'embellishers' of cloth with jewels carried high status. They were specialized craftsmen and better paid than most embroiderers. Thomasina Parker was a 'garnisshster' and was left a gift in the draper John Parker's will.

The design and embroidery on some of the best vestments and church furnishings was so fine it was like painting with a needle and was described as *acupictura*. The saints could be identified with their attributes or symbols so the holy stories could be easily understood, even by the illiterate. The design of the figures, draperies and gestures tended to be rather stylized, with the more important people depicted larger in size. The faces had large, intense black-ringed protruding eyes, high foreheads and wavy

Peter the Deacon, part of the set of stole and maniple given at the instigation of Queen Aelfflaed to St Cuthbert's shrine. Worked in Winchester on a silk ground in surface couching using pure gold wrapped around a silk core, split and stem stitches (909–918).
By permission of the Dean and Chapter Durham Cathedral.

hair worked in alternating shades of green and red or other unrealistic colours. Split stitch, tightly packed and shaded, was worked in spirals to show the contours of the face and figure, and great sensitivity and pathos was achieved in these delicate embroideries. The congregation was able to ponder on the holy mysteries as they watched the priest up at the altar, clothed in the dazzling vestments. The embroideries were designed to touch the hearts of the faithful, draw them closer to the Church and help them to identify with the life and passion of Christ and His saints.

Professional Embroiderers

The period 1250 to 1350 is known as the Golden Age of *Opus Anglicanum*, but it was also a period of transition. As some convents became swamped with requests and commissions for fine embroidery, the names of professional embroiderers started to appear in the public records. Between 1239 and 1245, Mabel of Bury St Edmund's name occurs twenty-four times in the household accounts of Henry III (1216–72). Mabel made many items of church regalia including an offertory veil which took three years to make, chasuble, apparels, stole, farons, amice, collars and cuffs, plus a banner for the King. He obviously trusted her judgment because he left the design of it to her. Payments were made for gold, pearls, silk and fringe and later an appraisal to establish her fee, was requested from the 'discreet men and women with a knowledge of embroidery' and 'the better workers of the City of London'. Mabel is not mentioned again until 1256 when the King visited her and commanded:

'Because Mabel of St Edmunds serves the King and Queen for a long time in the making of ecclesiastical ornaments . . . that the same Mabel be given six ells of cloth, appropriate to her (status), and the lining of a robe of rabbit fur'. This gift of clothes was quite usual, highly valued and most welcome.

Other master embroiderers were receiving major commissions. In 1253, Maud of Cantuaria (Canterbury) was paid for a set of embroidered apparels ordered by the King's half-sister Alice de Lusignan, and Maud de Benetleye was paid £27.11s.8d for sixteen broad and narrow orphreys. A little later Joan de Woburn earned sixty-four shillings for making two more orphreys. In 1302, Aleyse Darcy was paid three hundred marks for a large cloth embroidered in gold and silk and sold to Henry de Lacy, Earl of Lincoln. Rose de Burfors, wife of a London merchant, is mentioned in the City of London records of 1317 when she was owed one hundred marks by Queen Isabella for an embroidered choir cope. These are substantial contracts to named women, indicating that the women were most likely professional embroiderers with apprentices and a properly set up, secure workshop. They were financially able to undertake top quality work and satisfy the exacting needs of their wealthy clients.

During the thirteenth century, embroiderers and their families started to set up workshops and cluster around particular areas of the City of London. Historians Fitch, Frannson and Ekwall found family names associated with embroidery. Fitch notes textile workshops and the name *Settere* often occurring around the church of Mary le Bow Bred Street and All Hallows. William le Settere and John Heyroun, a '*settere*', were called upon to value a silk embroidered cope. Alexander Settere in 1307 received £10 from Sir Ponces Roandi, chaplain to Master William Testa, in payment of £40 for an embroidered choir cope. Other names include '*le Seur*', '*le Asseur*' and '*le Setter*', which Frannson suggests comes from *saietier*, the Old French word for a silk weaver, while Ekwall proposes that the word 'set' comes from Middle English '*setten*' and therefore refers to an embroiderer who sets or fixes stones or gems onto a garment. '*Seu*' is listed as the French verb to sew, working with a needle and thread, so Ralph le Seur of St Mary-at-Hill in 1288, and William le Seour of the same parish in 1291 were possibly occupational names.

Ceremonial robe, embroidered with heraldic lions and tied with gold braid and worn over a sideless surcoat, the deep armholes and bottom edged with fur. By 1446, this surcoat was rather old fashioned, a style mostly reserved for formal court occasions.

With increasing requests for top quality work, agents started to look to the cities for skilled embroiderers. In the past they had seen the nunneries as a source of cheap labour, but now they realized they could control these valuable commissions themselves. In 1251 Adam de Basing was described as an embroiderer, but he was probably an agent as well as a very successful London merchant and mayor. He supplied Henry III with fabric produced by Gerard le Bas in 1250 and a coat for £14.8s, so perhaps he financed other embroiderers as well. Matthew Paris may have been obliquely referring to Adam de Basing in his *Chronica Maiorum* when he wrote in 1246:

'My Lord Pope (Innocent IV 1243–54) noted the embroidered gold worked orphreys of the copes of certain English priests at the Council of Lyons in 1246, and commanded that the Cistercian abbots supply him with orphreys to ornament his copes and chasubles without delay, just as if they could be got for nothing and this did not displease the London merchants who traded in these embroideries and sold them at their own price'

This sounds as if Adam de Basing, rather than the embroiderers, benefited financially from the Pope's desire for these beautiful status symbols.

The Papal Treasury and Wardrobe Accounts give valuable information about continuing acquisition, patronage and gift-giving. Pope Urban IV (1261–1264) employed an English embroiderer, Gregory of London, who was especially skilled in gold work. The 1295 Papal inventory itemizes 113 pieces of *Opus Anglicanum*, more than any other kind of embroidery. Edward I sent a beautiful cope to Pope Nicholas VI and around 1295 he sent another to Pope Boniface VIII, both of *Opus Anglicanum*, which Pope Boniface later presented to local cathedrals. Pope John XXII (1316–34) received several valuable copes as gifts from England, including one sent in 1322 by the Archbishop of Canterbury and another, richly embroidered, sent by the Bishop of Ely in 1333. Edward II and Queen Isabella sent him another one on his accession, decorated with large pearls.

Setting up a large embroidery studio required access to credit, to import or purchase the silk, gold and jewels and pay the workers, so both Church and State were encouraged to offer patronage to ensure that their work got priority. These workshops spawned a whole new group of businessmen, managers and financiers who were already well established as middlemen, anticipating demand, facilitating production and satisfying the greed and competition for these beautiful

Syon cope, 1300–20. When the monastery at Syon was threatened during the Dissolution, the Brigantine nuns fled to Flanders, France and finally Portugal, taking with them their precious vestments. The entire linen ground is covered with underside couching in a chevron pattern, each quatrefoil containing a saint, angel or holy scene.
With permission of the V&A Museum, London.

textiles. Security was essential as gold and jewels needed locked vaults, while special chests and caskets were required to store the bolts of silk in clean, dry conditions. Silk floss was imported in bundles and then plied and doubled by the throwsters to give a particular weight and texture to the design. The Great Wardrobe accounts of 1333 note that silk thread was very expensive at fifteen shillings per pound compared with linen at only three shillings per pound. Silk thread was usually purchased from City mercers or Italian merchants who imported it in a wide range of colours, to match the dyed silk fabric they supplied. While the workshop probably had the embroidery frames, each worker seemed to have their own pins, needles and scissors as they are never mentioned in workshop lists.

A Time of Change

In fourteenth century London, there were other changes in the balance of working life, with more women being employed as workers in larger workshops, rather than being independent mistresses of their craft. In 1330, three counterpanes were made for

Philippa of Hainault and Edward III for the elaborate churching ceremonials following the birth of the Black Prince. Wardrobe accounts show two artist/designers, John de Kerdyff and John de Chidelee, heading a team of one hundred and twelve people. John de Kerdyff was probably in charge, as he was paid 8 1/8 pennies per day for seventy-two days, while John de Chidelee was only paid 6 ¼ pennies per day for the 78 days he was involved. Both men were described as a protractor, an artist or designer. The silk velvet for the counterpanes cost £72, and along with fourteen pounds of gold and sixteen pounds of silk thread, the total cost was £201.15s.5.3/4, more than many medieval workers might earn in a lifetime. Of the workforce, seventy men earned 4 ½ pennies per day, and forty-two women earned 3 ¼ pennies per day, a total of £60.17s.6d per day, a vast sum of money for the time.

Some embroiderers were journeymen and women who had completed their apprenticeship but could not afford to set up on their own, while others were partly skilled. One way or another, men were paid far more than women for the same job. It was believed that a woman should earn less otherwise it would upset the balance of the partnership, where man was the leader and woman the follower. Both the Church and State promoted laws and edicts, backed by selected passages from scripture, to ensure that these views were cast in stone. The women embroiderers were as highly skilled as the men, but their pay did not reflect this. By the time they became organized into a guild, it was too late to insist on equality of wages.

A big commercial workshop required highly skilled embroiderers, and many more semi-skilled workers, tailors and seamstresses, experienced in working with silk. Sometimes artists like John le Bonde and John de Stebenhethe worked together to supervise a large group. In 1308 they were described as Brouderers, but what is less clear is whether they actually picked up a needle or just supervised their workers. Sometimes, known artists like the two expert illuminators, Dame Margot and Dame Aales, were commissioned to design embroidery, but many master embroiderers probably did the designs as well. St Dunstan (c909–88), Archbishop of Canterbury, was an expert designer and was often called upon to design special vestments, but his regular visits to a pious woman called Eadelthrym to offer guidance, caused some caustic comment.

The iconography used to identify particular saints and holy stories was universal, and a good artist could take these common elements called attributes, and combine them afresh to fit the current style and requirements as requested by the patron. Pattern books were available, and were used over quite long periods by artists designing vestments and domestic furnishings. One dates from around 1280 and was still in use towards the end of the fourteenth century. Inspiration came from the Bible and the Book of Revelations, popular saints, the Apocrypha and the Life of the Virgin Mary. Everyday life, current literature and scenes from medieval romances were popular as were the Knights of the Round Table and hunting scenes, or a pun on the donor's name: a glove for the Glover family. Patterns included interlacing, acanthus, flowers, banderoles, inscriptions and mottoes, using both religious and secular motifs.

It was a chivalric age, a time of crusades and romantic ideals. Coats of arms and other signs and symbols of heraldry were used to give quick recognition on the battlefield or at tournaments. Sometimes symbols were used on ecclesiastical items, like the small repeating rampant lions on the Clare Chasuble (1272–94) and the John of Thanet panel (1300–20). The symbols were embroidered onto surcoats, horse trappings, banners and pennons, carried by the knights. Fashionable ladies carried tiny sheer silk banners called *oriflammes*, embroidered on both sides with a picture of the Virgin Mary or a likeness of themselves, a style of embroidery known as a *deux endroit*. Late in the fourteenth century, Gile Davynell earned over £700 for embroidering a jupon or military coat for the Black Prince, along with some other items. Embroiderers who could execute superior heraldic work could name their price and gain great prestige and profit.

The Great Period of *Opus Anglicanum* was passing and gradually and imperceptibly from the mid-thirteen-hundreds onwards, standards of craftsmanship began to deteriorate. This was due to the pressure put on the embroiderers by impatient and demanding clients, social and economic stress and the prolonged, expensive, civil and foreign wars of the later fourteenth and fifteenth centuries. Many highly skilled people died during the Black Death (1348-9) and those

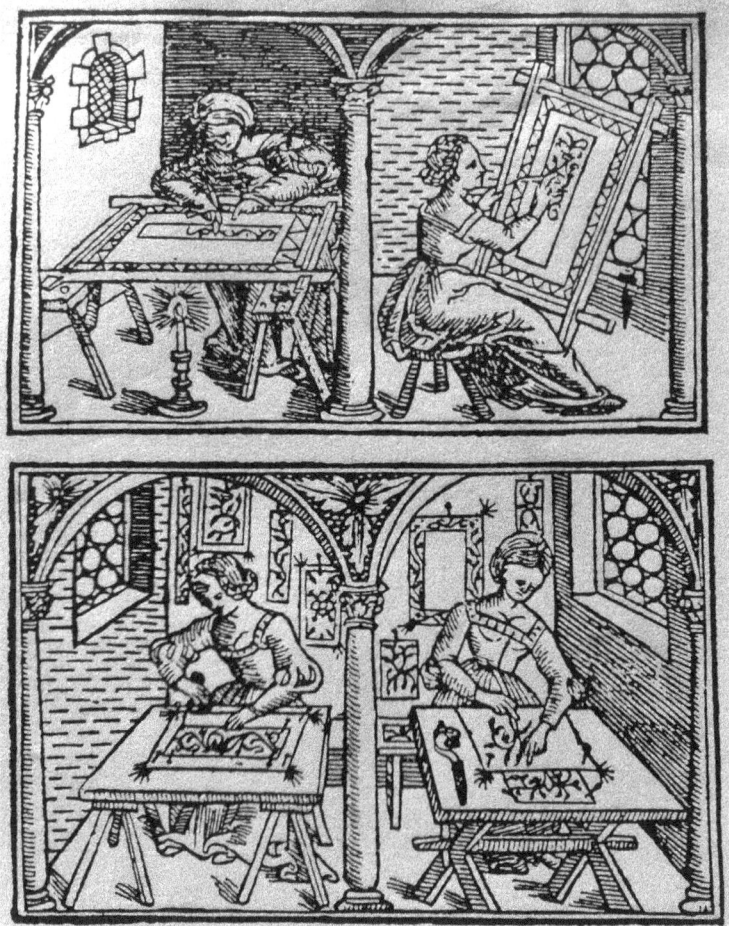

Four small scenes of embroiderers at work, pricking and pouncing, attaching the silk to a frame, transferring the design and embroidering. Windows and a candle remind of the need for good light although the guilds tried to stop people working in the evening.

that did survive often moved away or settled in other districts, so studios broke up and skills were lost. Church embroidery became formulaic, repeating a conventional design or motif, the pineapple, angels or fleur-de-lis. Production became geared to a price, and mass production methods and shortcuts were adopted in the large workshops. Stencilling or painting on a design was much faster and cheaper to produce than fine embroidery, and so was used on wall, bed and horse covers, banners and clothes, like those depicted in the Luttrell Psalter (1335–40).

Ladies embroidering, with the help of a mirror to focus the light, from the Cluny tapestries, early 16thc.

Changes in taste and a growing commercial sophistication, along with great advances in the manufacture of exquisite woven damasks, velvets, cloth of gold and other luxurious woven silks, meant that rich imported broad loom silks became very fashionable and sought after. Many semi-skilled embroiderers were now working in dire conditions, crouched over long tables in poor light and unhealthy surroundings, producing little stacks of standard designs of saints and flowers, scenes from scripture and holy stories. These embroidered slips were produced in their hundreds and available for a patron to just choose from stock. The slips were then appliqued onto the silk damask, and a braid edging and a light dusting of fancy stitches or perhaps a family shield were added to personalize the item and tie the design together, as in the Erpingham Chasuble (early fifteenth century). These techniques were less durable than split stitch or couching, and never so highly esteemed, and gradually both ecclesiastical and secular embroidery grew coarser. By the end of the Middle Ages, the centre of production of the finest embroidery had passed from England to the Continent.

Maidens collecting silkworms and weaving silk, from the story of Pamphile by Boccaccio in *De claris mulieribus*, MS Royal 16 Gv, f.54v French, Fifteenth century, British Library, London.

CHAPTER FIVE
The Medieval Silk-women

The silk-women of London were real women with personalities, achievements, anxieties and ambitions. Their actual correspondence in some cases can still be read, their signature on deeds still clear and firm. It was a smallish world. They lived in the same area, and married within their close circle of friends, neighbours and associates. They stood surety for each other, were godparents to each other's children, helped one another with large orders and joined together to protect themselves, even petitioning the King when they felt their livelihood was being threatened.

Some London women took the opportunity to get into a luxury trade, by turning their domestic skill for spinning wool into spinning silk, a high value item for the increasingly exotic needs and demands of the rising city merchants, the court and the Church. Silk was then given added value by weaving it into narrow ribbons and braids, wrapping it with gold to make thread for embroidery and making it into fashion items, hats, gloves, purses, hairnets, fringes and tassels. Some women took the imported silk fabric and embroidered it with silk floss to make bags, alms purses and gifts. Working with silk was considered highly skilled women's work, and a prestigious craft.

Most craft and merchant households were based around a married couple, their children, apprentices, servants and dependents, directed by the most senior man in the family. Women raised their children, took care of the preparation of food and clothing and assisted their husbands in their trades. Families had always worked

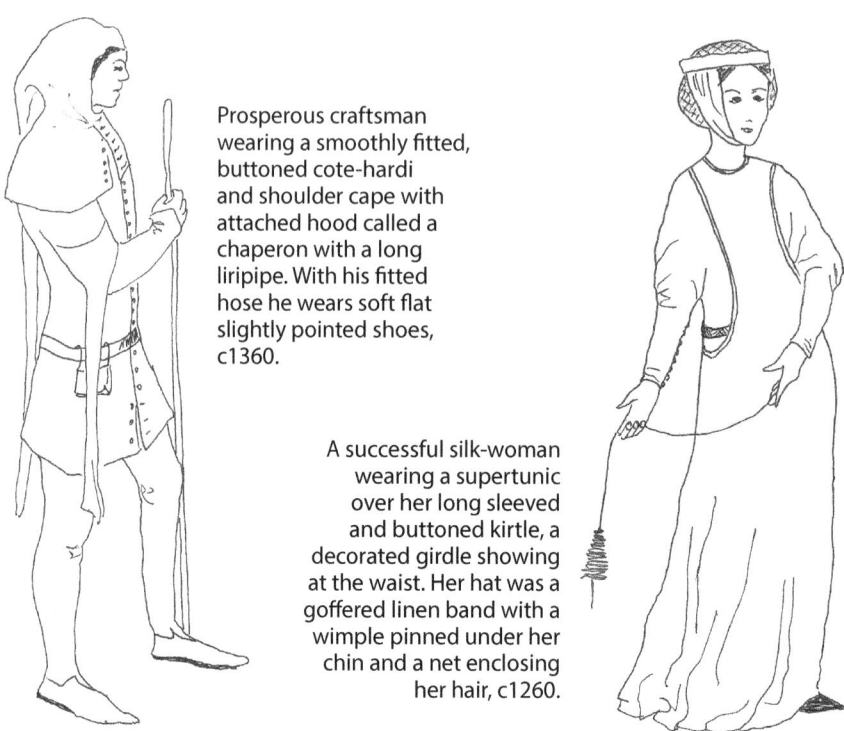

Prosperous craftsman wearing a smoothly fitted, buttoned cote-hardi and shoulder cape with attached hood called a chaperon with a long liripipe. With his fitted hose he wears soft flat slightly pointed shoes, c1360.

A successful silk-woman wearing a supertunic over her long sleeved and buttoned kirtle, a decorated girdle showing at the waist. Her hat was a goffered linen band with a wimple pinned under her chin and a net enclosing her hair, c1260.

together, cooperating and supporting each other within their domestic and parish sphere. It was a flexible and traditional division of labour, but still gender specific.

The majority of medieval silk-women worked the silk in their own homes, supplying other silk-women with spun or thrown silk on order. Sometimes it was an agent who supplied the raw silk, even the equipment, spindle or spinning wheel. These silk-women were in effect outworkers, offering their work in exchange for a small wage to supplement their families' incomes. They taught their daughters who also contributed to the welfare of the family as unpaid labour until they married. For the more accomplished silk-woman, it was not merely a sideline to her domestic duties; she was mistress of her craft. These silk-women were recognized as being highly skilled craftswomen and some became very successful businesswomen, traders, importing silk, organizing other workers and arranging lucrative contracts.

Successful silk-women had real standing in the city and being apprenticed to a silk mistress improved a girl's chance to marry well. Quite a lot is known about Alice Claver; it seems that after she had completed her apprenticeship to a London silk-woman, to learn the 'misteries of sylkework', she married well, becoming the second wife of a successful mercer and guildsman, Richard Claver. Another woman described herself in the records as a throwster and both of her husbands were wealthy goldsmiths, the second one becoming an alderman.

Business success often came from the combination of the husband's commercial ability and position in his guild and his wife's expertise and success as a silk-woman. As a member of one of the major textile craft guilds — the mercers, drapers, haberdashers, embroiderers, or the prestigious goldsmiths or Merchant Adventurers — he could supply his wife with all the silk she needed, deal with the contracts, imports and exports and raise the finance. His knowledge of the City and contacts with the Italian merchants who imported the various grades of silk, meant a husband and wife could become economically powerful. Other craftspeople came to depend on them to provide them with the raw silk, and often to employ them too. Without his wife Elizabeth's financial support from her very successful silk business, John Stokton would have found it harder to rise to the highest position in the city, that of Lord Mayor of London. It was very expensive for a man to be an office holder in the city or his guild. Although these powerful positions had great prestige and some minor advantages, they were unpaid.

The silk-women formed a network of friends and colleagues and called on each other for help and advice. They all lived near the Guildhall around Soper Lane, Milk Street, Cheapside and St Lawrence Jewry and adjoining parishes. Alice Claver's closest friend, her 'gossep', was Alice Bothe, who lived nearby in the parish of St Mary Aldermanbury. A gossep indicated a more intimate and trusted friendship, often with godchildren in common. Their husbands were both mercers, handling a wide range of textiles and haberdashery. After Richard Claver died in 1456, Alice often called on William Pratte, Alice Bothe's husband, for help. There were still some areas, like raising larger amounts of finance, that were out of the range of women, even very successful businesswomen. Beatrice Fyler was another friend of Elizabeth and the two Alice's. She lived nearby in Milk Street in the parish of St Mary Magdalene with her husband Thomas Fyler, also a mercer, and their eight children. The women trusted each other's integrity and ability even to the extent of acting as executrix to each other's wills.

When she died, Beatrice left her business and £50 to her eldest son Edward and £30 to each of her unmarried daughters, but Edward died soon after. In his will he left bequests to a number of women, probably former apprentices or employees of Beatrice, including Catherine Sergeaunt, twenty shillings, Alice Andrew, twenty shillings, Anne Dolfynby, ten shillings and Joan Stokes, £4. All were carefully named and the bequests noted. Beatrice's daughter Joan Marshall, also a silk-woman, probably continued to provide work for these women who had depended upon her mother.

The work

Spinning and throwing were women's work and it was rare to find a male spinner or throwster turning raw silk into yarn. A spindle was used and preferred for the finest thread, even after the spinning wheel became available during the thirteenth century. The colour and quality of the silk thread varied, depending on the quality of the raw silk and the skill of the spinner.

The silk weavers wove narrow wares, braid, ribbons, girdles or corses, laces, cauls and nets for the hair, fringes, tassels and buttons. Cauls and other woven silk fragments have been found in London excavations, including four examples of hairnets, one from the thirteenth century, and three from the fourteenth. The later ones were made of fine handknotted silk mesh, heavy enough to support jewels and other decorations. These hairnets were made using a long narrow netting needle, usually of copper alloy with an eye at each end. A bone weaving tablet, with four holes through which threads pass to build up the pattern, was found in a Fenchurch Street deposit and offered conclusive evidence that braids had been woven in Britain since the time of the Roman occupation. Braid and ribbon making was women's work. It required little space or equipment, just a set of tablets or a small box loom with rigid heddles through which the silk warp was threaded. There were four main types of braid: tablet woven, tabby weave, finger-looped and plaited. The silk was usually plied and then doubled up to five threads for strength. It was a popular craft and vast numbers of elaborate gold and silver braids and ribbons were made by silk-women in their own homes, or in workshops established under the patronage of the court and Church.

Occasionally silk was knitted to make ecclesiastical gloves, although silk stockings were probably not knitted in Britain until the sixteenth century. Many women made silk fashion accessories, but major items of clothing, both secular and ecclesiastical, were made by tailors. The women were prevented from making whole garments by guild regulations, designed to protect men's work, although the women possibly made the bed linen and clothes for their family.

The traditional way to learn a trade was to be apprenticed. When Alice Bothe came to London from Derby, she lived in the house of John Abbot in Catte Street and was probably apprenticed to his wife who was a silk-woman. Abbot was a mercer and Alice met her future husband William Pratte while he was apprenticed to Abbot. It was during these years that Alice and William began a fifty-year friendship with another mercer and future printer, William Caxton.

Apprenticeships were an integral part of city life. Some girls were apprenticed to silk-women to learn all aspects of silk work, while others were bound to women who were distinguished in a particular area, like throwing silk or weaving corses. The girls were bound by an indenture between their parents or guardians and their future mistress. A London ordinance of the early fifteenth century states that if:

> *'Those married women that are accustomed to practice certain crafts in the city by themselves without their husbands, are to take the girl as apprentice, to serve them and to learn their crafts, then these apprentices are to be bound in service by indentures of apprenticeship to both the husband and the wife in order to follow the mistery of the wife'.*

The girls came to London from as far away as Warwickshire and Yorkshire, Norfolk, Bristol, Buckinghamshire, Lincolnshire and Derby. A silk apprenticeship was usually for a term of seven to ten years, depending on the age of the girl when she was indentured. The terms were strict and she had a duty to cherish the interests of her mistress, not to waste the goods or merchandise or take them without permission, to behave well and not to frequent taverns and public houses, wander off or withdraw unlawfully from service. The mistress in turn promised to teach her and take charge and instruct her, to chastise her 'for her own good', and to give her sufficient food, clothing, footwear, a bed, and all other suitable necessities.

Deeds don't usually mention any payment, but on one occasion in the mid-sixteenth century a plea of debt was recorded by Marjery Rippyngale for £5 against a girl for board. The girl declared it was contrary to the agreement made to her mother, which arranged for the mistress to teach her 'the crafte and misterie of a Silkewoman & sewing' wherein she was 'expert and Connyng' finding the girl 'mete and drynke and all other things convenyent.' The girl's mother was to pay twenty shillings yearly to William and Marjery Rippyngale and the girl was to do service for her board. The insistence that she do service, presumably the work of a servant, as well as pay a fee to learn her trade, suggests something rather different from the usual apprenticeship.

Daughter of the house. She helped with the household chores and was taught by her mother to spin, contributing to the family's income and standard of living until she married.

As well as being constantly on hand to help and learn the techniques of working with silk, the girls were often entrusted with money and sent on various errands, delivering silk and making purchases. There was a celebrated case which led to recriminations and accusations that continued for twelve years. Joan Woulbarowe maintained that her mistress Katherine Dore 'immagening sotelly to haue hold vppon her' had forced her to remain in service when her apprenticeship had finished, and then had her imprisoned until she could pay back £12.13s.4d which Katherine maintained she was owed. Of this money, £8 was the value of silk items which Joan had delivered to two women 'custumers & werkers of ye said Katherine' who were living in Soper Lane. Katherine maintained that her apprentice had unjustly taken 'thowen sylke, vncoloued and sylke dyed' amounting to £12.4s 10d, whereas Joan stated that Katherine had long since recovered her goods. In addition Katherine said that Joan still owed

Man instructing woman in the working of the spinning wheel, much to her chagrin, Royal MS. British Library.

Cat 'helping' a nun with her spinning, MS British Library.

The Medieval Silk-women

her £7.10s which Joan had paid to various people 'in the tyme of her Prentyshode brought silke by the Commaundement' and for the use of her mistress. The whole business had become quite unpleasant and was in dispute over two court terms, until it was finally decided in Joan's favour.

Thankfully most apprenticeships worked well and at completion, the silk-women had their apprentices' names formally recorded by the City of London. Some girls were greatly cherished and left items in wills. In 1456, a silk-woman called Isabel Fremely left a pair of sheets and her girdle of green silk garnished with silver to her apprentice. Agnes Brundyssch, a 'citizen and silk-woman' of London, said she released Alice Seford from the rest of her term of apprenticeship and left her some household goods as well. Alice Claver had a series of apprentices over thirty years, although Margaret Taillour is the only woman specifically designated as her apprentice in her will and she received twenty shillings. Elizabeth Bertram was a 'cosen' of Alice's late husband Richard and she was described as her servant, although she was probably an ex-apprentice and Alice generously left her a bequest of ten marks. Elizabeth Atkynson was another 'servant', again possibly an ex-apprentice, who received the lesser amount of 53s. 4d. The official records note surprisingly few apprenticeships. Of the 123 silk-women named in the period between 1300 and 1500, only twelve apprenticeships were registered. The silk-women did not form a guild, so probably most arrangements were informal.

Feme Couverte de Baron and Feme Sole

Once an apprenticeship was complete and the young woman had worked for a year and a day she was free to work on her own account. However, she was unlikely, to have the business skills or capital to afford to marry or set up her own shop. Many young silk-women continued to work for their former mistress for wages until they married and moved to their husband's house. From there they would supply an agent or work their silk on a small scale. The large capital outlay required to take premises, act as an employer with apprentices and sell both wholesale and retail, was beyond the possibilities for most.

Woodcut of a marriage before a priest and witnesses, by Gunther Zainer, Augsburg 1477, in: Albert Schramm, *Der Biblderschmuck der Fruhdrucke*, Vol II, Leipzig, 1920.

Those silk-women who married well, and had the financial backing and support of their husbands, would probably work as a '*feme couverte de baron*', working under the 'cover' or protection of their husbands. A woman was traditionally and in law the property of her husband, and he was financially responsible for all her debts. As a guildsman and master craftsman he could be of great assistance to his wife as he had better access to commercial contacts, imported materials and finance. London Chancery Proceedings note that wives who traded in the city were a normal occurrence.

Some widows and single women, even some married women, once they could afford to present themselves before the Mayor and Aldermen and prove that they were successful, of high moral standing and financially able to honour their debts and commitments, could then apply to become a '*feme sole*', a single trader. It was a very serious step to take, to move beyond the care and protection of her husband, and a London Act of 1340 in Book III of the *Liber Albus* states:

'Where a woman couverte de baron follows any craft within the city by herself apart, with which the husband in no way intermeddles, such a woman should be bound as a single woman as to all that concerns her said craft. And if the husband and wife are impleaded, in such case the wife shall plead as a single woman in a Court of Record, and shall have her law and other advantages by way of plea just as a single woman. And if she is condemned, she shall be committed to prison until she shall have made satisfaction; and neither the husband nor his goods shall in such a case be charged or interfered with.'

In addition to renting a shop or place of work, as a sole trader she could buy and sell all types of merchandise and swear oaths in the courts. She could arrange contracts and act independently, as if her husband had left the country permanently, entered a religious house or died, and as though she were a single woman or widow and not merely a chattel of her husband. In the eyes of the church she was still a married woman. These privileges and advantages were entirely economic, with no political rights. The custom of male guardianship survived into the late Middle Ages and women, both single and married, like children, had no civil status, with no legal and separate existence or property of their own, until they were widowed.

In the year 1457, the Guildhall Journal records only two silk-women who came before the Mayor of London and declared that they were sole merchants, yet both women said that they had done so for a long time. Perhaps they wanted to work on a larger scale than before and raise finance or import silk from abroad. In reality, most silk-women probably remained *'couverte de baron'*, with their husband responsible for payment of their debts although it is known that Alice Claver, Beatrice Fyler and Elizabeth Stokton were all trading as *feme sole*.

Most women trading as a *feme sole* were successful, but there were cases where a merchant had sold a considerable amount of silk to a silk-woman and had been unable to recover the debt because there was no record that she had ever been formally admitted as a sole merchant. Johanne Horne, the wife of William Horne, a saddler and Alderman of London, had used her seal and affirmed to Sir John Ffynkell a mercer, that she was a sole merchant when, in the 1490s,

Successful businessman, c1400 wearing a long houppelande with a high neck and deep bag sleeves that doubled as a useful pocket. The more prosperous he was the better the quality of the dyed fabric.

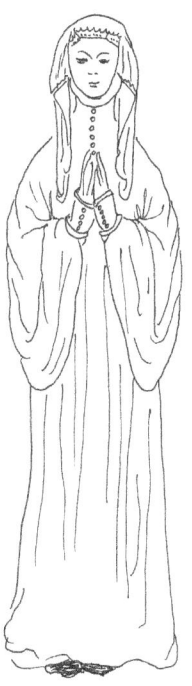

Woman wearing the practical and comfortable full length houppelande. A married woman modestly wore hers buttoned up to the neck, her hair covered and the long sleeves of her under dress covering her knuckles. c1400.

she purchased silk from him worth £56.0s.6d. Ffynkell feared that if she was not registered as a *feme sole*, then his case would follow common law, and he would not be able to reclaim the debt.

Alice Claver continued to practice her craft after her marriage and probably did so initially as a *couverte de baron* with her husband Richard's consent and support. Richard was twenty years older than Alice, and when he died within five years of their marriage his will states lovingly: 'and all waye I praye yowe, tender my wyff well for she hath ben to me a full luffyng woman en my sekeness ther God reward her en hevyn for that sche hath be to me'. It is not known for sure when Alice started trading as a *feme sole*, but probably before Richard died because he fully appreciated her ability and integrity. He named her one of the executors of his will and left her the guardianship of their little son Richard, and the considerable sum of £200, along with his household goods and 'her own goodys'.

Imports & Exports

Raw silk was imported into London, Dover, Southampton and other British ports in many forms, including loosely wrapped bundles described as 'papers of silk ', or in long wrapped skeins called fardels. There was little consistency in the size of the bundles or their weight. A fardel varied in price from £30.18s.9d to £57.12s. Leonard Conterin is known to have sold silk to eight women during one year and each fardel was of a different weight and value.

This raw silk could be further processed or sold as a finished article or as sewing silk. The Italian importers and the City merchants supplied a wide range of different silk threads, often dyed to match the silk fabric they imported. Private women like the Paston women of Norfolk, sometimes bought a fine two-ply thread for eyelets, buttonholes and topstitching. Some silk was supplied on a tube, like the 'gold of Cyprus on a pipe'. It was bought by Isabel Norman 'trading for herself in the craft of silk-woman', from a Genoese merchant through David Galganete who acted as a broker between them. Between the 18th and 22nd years of Henry VI's reign, twenty-three women bought silk from foreigners, mostly the Venetians.

As well as buying silk from the London merchants, some women, probably mostly widows, did travel long distances on business. They would need to have been relatively free of home responsibilities and family demands. Competing in a bigger world required special knowledge and a sharp business acumen, capital and commitment. These silk-women mixed with people outside their known society, and this caused some anxiety. Some men feared that her experiences would give her added status and authority and could be a direct challenge to their view of themselves as the leaders in the field.

Some women like Jane Langton figure a number of times in Chancery Proceedings and the Great Wardrobe Accounts, the King's powerful household department, as trading in larger quantities of goods. After her daughter-in-law Agnes died at the Stourbridge Fair, Jane agreed to be bound for payment for corses of gold and silk goods to the substantial value of £300.15s. Despite this assurance, the agents of the two merchants of Genoa had her arrested to ensure they were paid, but she maintained she had sufficient goods and funds to cover the debt, anyway. It was usual for families to share a debt and in 1503, not long after the problems with the Genoese merchants, Jane Langton's son John and his second wife Elizabeth were supplying quantities of silk and other goods amounting to £101.17s.5 ¼ p for members of the Royal Family. Two years later in 1505, the Great Wardrobe paid Jane Langton for various purchases, for the use of 'the Lady Mary'.

1 oz of 'open silk' of divers colours — 16d
(possibly coloured weft threads, composed
of two or three strands of unthrown silk)

1 oz of 'Twyne silk' of divers colours — 16d

1 oz of Venice gold — 4s

1 'weaving stole cum sleys pro eodem' — 3s

1 oz 'webbe silk' — 16d
(possibly lightly twisted tram)

'a quarter hedelyng threde pro le webbe' — 5d
(loops of filament silk that hung on the
loom through which the warp threads passed)

1 oz of gold 'de damask' — 5s

Piece goods are first mentioned in connection with the Act of the 19th year of Henry VII's reign which stated that no person might import into England for sale

> *'eny manner of Sykle, wrought by hyt selfe or wt eny other stuffe in eny place out of this Realme, in Ribandes laces gyrdylles Corses Calles (a fine hair net) Corss of tissues or poyntes,' but gave at the same time freedom to any person, ' denzien or stranger, to import al other manner of Syklkes, as well wrought as rawe, or unwrought to sell at pleasour'.*

The Silk-women's Petitions

It was just these kinds of problems that had led the silk-women over one hundred years earlier to get together to present a petition to the Lord Mayor against a Lombard who was cornering the market for all the raw and coloured silk. Although a London Silk-women's Guild was never formalized, the silk workers were sufficiently organized by '. . . Wednesday after the Feast of St Katherine' (25 November 1368) when some 'Silkwymmen' delivered to the Mayor and Aldermen a bill complaining that fifteen days earlier a pound of raw silk *(soie crude)* was worth fourteen shillings, but Nicholas Sarduche, a Lombard, by his 'crafty and evil design' had seized all the silk that he could find for sale in London and refused to sell it for less than eighteen shillings. Further, 'he daily spied out all the aliens bringing such merchandise to London' and there he either commandeered the market or caused them to sell it all at a higher price than they would otherwise have done, 'to the great damage of the said women and the whole realm'. Therefore 'the complainant prayed for a remedy, that they might not have cause to complain elsewhere'.

On being questioned on the 2nd December 1368, Nicholas Sarduche maintained that his master and partners had warned him by letter that 'divers bales of silk and other merchandise' had been lost and stolen on their way to Bruges, and they thought the price of silk would rise in future and that he should buy as much silk as he could. In fact, he had bought all the silk he could find, both to sell in the city at a profit and to export abroad for resale. He was not aware that he had done anything wrong in doing so and he was willing to sell the silk to anyone at all, at sixteen shillings a pound.

He was then asked by the court what quantity of silk he had bought and from whom and where it was weighed. He said he had bought fifty-nine pounds of raw silk from Paul Penyk, a Lombard, and eighty pounds of coloured silk from Dyne Sanoche, another Lombard. He admitted that all of his silk was weighed in his own house on his own balance, and not by the common balance of the city. This caused a great upset because it was against the law not to use the City's small weighing beam, and it was widely believed that Sarduche's balance was inaccurately weighted in his favour.

The court did not believe his story and he was imprisoned and his goods forfeited.

Lombards and other unspecified 'aliens' were constantly being accused of destroying the livelihood of the silk-women by importing into England 'silk thrown Rybens, and laces falsely and decyrably wrought, and corses of silke'. Between 1455 and 1504 there were five successful petitions to protect their work against foreign competition. Silk-women like Beatrice Fyler, Joan Marshall-Fyler, and Elizabeth Stokton probably took an active part in the politics of their craft, but Alice Claver was unlikely to have been involved in the silk-women's petition of 1455, as her husband would have been ill by that time. The petition was repeated with few changes in 1463:

> *'Silkewomen and throwesters of the craftes and occupation of silkework within London, which be and have been craftes of women within the same cite, of tyme that noo mynde renneth unto the contrary . . . many a wurshipfull woman . . have lyved full honourably, and theirwith many good housholdes kepte, and many gentliwomen, and other in grete nombre, . . . have been drawen under theym in lernyng the same craftes . . . full vertuously unto the plesaunce of God.'*

The silk-women maintained that the Lombards and other foreigners wanted to destroy these crafts, 'and all such vertueux occupations for wymmen with yis lande'. They thought the Lombards were trying to become rich and powerful by importing ready-made silk items and controlling the price of silk, thereby taking away the silk-women's livelihood. The women complained that they could not make the products themselves because only poor quality unwrought or raw silk was being brought into England. They asked Parliament to ask the King to ban all finished silk from coming into England, and this request was granted.

Twenty years later, men are mentioned for the first time in connection with silk work in the petition of 1482 which says there were 'menne and women of the hole craft of Silkewerk of the Cite of London and all other Citeis, Townes, Boroghes and Vilages of this Realme of Englond.'. Perhaps these were men who had taken

Woman caring for her child and guiding him in a baby walker. German woodcut, Printed by Heinrich Laufenberg, Augsburg 1491, in: Albert Schramm, Der Bilderschmuck der Fruhdrucke, Vol XXIII, Leipzig, 1943.

over running the silk-women's businesses or men who assisted wives who either found it unnecessary to trade *sole* or were not permitted to do so by their husbands. If the men were guildsmen or aldermen, their knowledge of the City would have been invaluable in petitioning the King. The alien merchants were now defined as Jews and Saracens, and an embargo was set for four years and the penalty was forfeiture.

Alice Claver seems to be typical of the energetic and responsible silk-women of her time. It was a very busy life with a network of friends and business associates, both men and women. Her strong-mindedness made her business prosper to the extent of accepting many royal commissions over a long period. She belonged to parish fraternities, contributed to charities and made substantial gifts to her workers and ex-apprentices. Katherine Champyon was probably an ex-apprentice and was both loved and valued. She was Alice's

Lady tapestry weaving, using an upright frame. Her veiled hennin headdress, rich silk satin gown, carved stool and pleasant workspace all indicate a lady, rather than just a woman of the household. She has her yarns in the baskets and is weaving the design known as mille fleurs.

sole executrix and inherited the silk business and the residue of the entire estate. As a mark of respect and commitment to continuing this successful business, Katherine took the name Claver, as appears when she sold ribbon and thread to the Great Wardrobe in 1483 and 1485.

For the successful silk-woman who had a network of friends, family and men of influence, the need for a formal guild structure was not apparent. Unfortunately, forces were already at work that would result in the collapse of the silk-woman's life as she knew it.

Johan Lambard (d 1487) and his wife Ann, (d 1488), and six of their children. He was a Master silk merchant, and wears his fur lined Alderman's robes and tunic underneath, belt and gypciere or purse at the waist. Ann wears a fashionable headdress, fitted full-skirted dress with wide fur collar, a pomander hanging from her belt.

Brass, by kind permission of the Parochial Church Council of St Nicholas, Hinxworth, Herts.

CHAPTER SIX

The Guilds

In the Middle Ages the guilds were a major institution, a power base, a means of acquiring skills, wealth and prestige. All the major crafts formed themselves into guilds to establish an apprenticeship system to train young craftsmen, control their members and enforce quality standards over all the goods produced. The craftsmen got together for mutual support and fellowship and some guilds became very powerful. The London silk-women were unique in that they continued to function as the 'Sylkewymmen and Throwsters of the Crafts and Occupation of Silkewerk ', but never formalized into a guild, and by the end of the fifteenth century they had all but disappeared.

The successive visitations of the plague from 1348 left many people dead, families depleted and traumatized. Of those who did live through it, many left their homes and villages, drawn to the towns and cities, especially London, seeking a fresh start. They were looking for work and to make their fortune, free from the entrenched restrictions of village life, tied to their lord and the land. It cannot have been easy to establish oneself in this wider world and not everyone succeeded.

In London the new arrivals gathered together with men working in similar trades. They joined older masters and gradually earned the right to become a member of one of the craft guilds or confraternities. The guilds created statutes and regulations with an extensive symbolism of tools, patron saints and civic pageantry and issued regulations to cover all aspects of their trade.

As well as the craft guilds, there was another group of prosperous established businessmen who formed themselves into merchant guilds. They were prepared to pay a tax or geld to the Crown, to protect their monopolies and privileges. The *Gilda Mercatoria*, were the merchant guilds and initially included craftsmen. Later they became the *Gilda Mercatorum* or guild-merchants, and limited their members to established dealers and traders in their field. Some of these guilds, companies and liveries started as parish fraternities, associations of people seeking to secure mutual support and fellowship during their life, and prayers for their souls after death. They moved in more elevated circles, with an extensive network of friends and colleagues, acquiring contacts among the hierarchy of the church and court. They developed elements of secrecy and symbolism, wore distinctive dress or livery, and fought hard to have their privileges endorsed by the court. As trade intensified, the merchants gained greater prestige and became more powerful. By the early 1300s they had become exclusive trading fraternities.

The structure and scale, limitations and opportunities for the London silk market, rested with the drive and fortune of the merchants and the middle-men of the Merchant Guilds and Livery Companies. They controlled the capital, finance, import and distribution of the raw silk from Asia, the Middle East and Europe. From the ninth century, Byzantine silk had been traded in London and York and by the fourteenth century, London had become as important an international commercial centre for the silk trade as Venice, Genoa, Marseilles, Paris and Cologne.

In Britain wool was paramount. The Spitalfields Worshipful Company of Weavers was founded in London in 1155, and was granted a Charter by Henry II (1133–89). With its strict rules on personal, civic and social behaviour and insistence on high standards of workmanship and every aspect of the craft, it became the prototype for English Medieval Guilds. The members were weavers of wool, not silk. There is no evidence that broad loom silks were woven in London, neither the fancy satins, brocades and velvets, nor the fine gauze for veils. These were all imported from

Guildsman & wife, both are wearing fine houppelandes edged with fur, his large purse and her silk under dress and gold crespine hair net show their success and standing in their Guild, fragment from the Tree of Consanguinity Loyset Liedet Fr 1471 Biblio Nat Paris.

The Guilds 105

the European silk manufacturing centres especially Venice, Lucca, Genoa and Florence. There was a brief attempt, promoted by King Edward IV (1442–83), to set up silk weaving in London. An Italian weaver, Gefferay Damico who had 'konnyng and experience of wevyng clothes of damsakes, velwettys, cloth of gold, and other clothes of sylk ', was offered a house in Westminster so he could weave silk and teach these skills. This seems to have aroused suspicion and opposition from the merchants and other silk importers, and Damico was hounded and later arrested on charges of debt and trespass, which brought the experiment effectively to an end.

The men of the prestigious Mercers Guild were ever watchful of anyone other than themselves importing silk into the country, and they were especially antagonistic towards the Italians and the members of the Hanseatic trading league. These foreign merchants, known as 'aliens' sometimes prospered under aristocratic patronage or church support, but the local merchants were often hostile, forcing alien merchants to deal in a particular area of the town through specific channels and brokers. In 1480, William Pratte and some of the other mercers had prepared a 'book' on the offences of the Hanse to put before the King's Council. It is most likely that William Pratte and the other husbands of the silk-women, with their expertise in drafting reports, were also involved with drawing up the various Petitions that the silk-women presented to the King, regarding the infringements by the aliens on their silk products.

It might be supposed that the members of the Mercers' Company were the natural protectors of the silk-women and would have been determined to block these imported goods, but in fact silk was only one part of their business. There could even have been a conflict of interest, because some of the silk-women were themselves silk importers competing against the mercers, although the amount involved was very small compared to that handled by the guildsmen. Some men were rather antagonistic towards the businesswomen and feared that if they led successful and public commercial lives, they would gain independent status. This, they thought, could have weakened the balance between men and women's work. Some feared the loss of their place at the head of the family if their wife worked on her own account with apprentices, servants or worse, handled her own money.

Sophisticated large patterned silk velvets and damasks featuring artichokes, vine leaves and pomegranates, the choice of Mayors and Aldermen for their robes to display their wealth and success.

Guilds were not egalitarian; they were male communities where women had little or no part. They had a strict hierarchy and the masters had the greatest prestige. They were men who had not only completed their apprenticeships, but had also become very successful. Under them were the journeymen or bachelors, of whatever age, who had completed their apprenticeship but still worked for wages. The apprentices and the Master guildsman's family were under them. Some guilds offered wives membership as 'sisters'. They usually paid lower membership fees, were able to take part in some of the religious and social events, but were barred from wearing livery or any serious decision making in the guild. Some guilds had women members, wives or associates, although key guilds like the scholars, lawyers, notaries, goldsmiths and portrait painters would not admit women under any circumstances.

Many of the guildsmen in the textile trades were married to silk-women and lived in the area near the Guildhall in the parish of St Lawrence Jewry where Alice Claver spent her widowhood. Richard Claver had lived with his first wife in the parish of St Michael Bassinshaw, near St Mary Aldermanbury, the home parish of his friends and the executors of his will, John Burton and John Stokton. Sir John Stokton was also a mercer, alderman and for a time, mayor of London, and was knighted for his part in the defense of the city against the Bastard of Fauconberg. After his death in 1473, Elizabeth Stokton married Gerard Caniziani, who was a representative of the Medici family. He was also a mercer and probably one of the silk-women's main suppliers of Italian silk. John Norlong, Ralph Kempe and William Pratte were all middling rank mercers and as neighbours and parishioners they helped and advised each other, supported their parish charities, witnessed each other's wills, and acted as executors. Until his death in 1486, William Pratte was very involved with his two companies: the Mercers and the Merchant Adventurers, serving as warden of the Mercers and as a councilman for the ward of Cripplegate.

It was a period of upward mobility. With increasing affluence and the rise of the middle classes, it was important that all should know of a man's success. The guild Masters took every opportunity to display their frequent and ever more extravagant changes of livery. They wore outer robes of purple, scarlet or green, furred with ermine, beaver and marten. They paraded resplendent in tunics of white samite and velvet, with silk-lined hoods trimmed with fur or gold thread embroidery. They wore brightly coloured striped silks, silken girdles and carried silk taffeta bags and purses. Even the lesser merchants had robes of silk edged with fur, but the Lord Mayor's regalia was the most magnificent of all: shot silk, rich velvets and cloth of gold, embellished with gold braid and jewels. Women seemed to have fewer gowns than their husbands. It was the men who were the peacocks.

Widowed Businesswomen in the Silk Trade

London widows had their own privileges and obligations. As the widow of a successful London mercer, Alice Claver could continue her husband's business for life, or until she remarried, and not just for forty days, as was more usual in the rest of England. Richard's death gave her back her separate legal persona, and as a widow of a Master craftsman and freeman she was entitled to be a freewoman, a *franche homme (feme)* of the city, provided she did not remarry.

Woodcut of a woman trader, selling clothes, some possibly secondhand. She wears a couvre-chef and apron, with a purse at her belt. A substantial stand with a mirror, suggests that this is her regular trade.
Woodcut, printed by Hans Hofmann, Nuremberg, 1490, in: Albert Schramm, *Der Biblderschmuck der Fruhdrucke*. Vol XVIII, Leipzig, 1935.

She could join in the economic and social life of the guild, although she was excluded from their political activities, and could not vote or serve as a guild officer. She could now run her late husband's business independently after paying a fee, and supervise the shop and apprentices. She could also have her name inscribed in the civic records and her will enrolled in the Court of Hustings. When trading outside the city, she would have privileges in other towns and markets. The conflict came when she had to decide whether to remain in her late husband's trade, and abandon her silk work, or to continue as a silk-woman without the support of his guild.

Widows' rights were a minefield, and they could be withdrawn for lots of reasons. The main one was her remarriage to a man who was not a member of the same guild or was a Master of another craft. The guildsmen feared that there could be a conflict of interest and worse, he might gain irregular access to her late husband's guild and be party to its secrets without the years of apprenticeship and training.

Alice Claver never remarried and remained a *feme sole* and master silk-woman in her own right. She was a widow for 33 years, so perhaps being a *mulier mercatrix sola*, a single businesswoman and trader, best suited her. Her business must have been a substantial one, and living near the Guildhall, she was ideally placed for the passing trade of rich officials, lawyers, merchants and representatives of livery companies, church and court. Her involvement in the charitable fraternities of her parish meant she knew many important, wealthy and powerful people, who were well able to afford her luxury goods.

The prestige of working for the crown would certainly have increased her business, as citizens and their wives were eager to patronize those who supplied royalty. The 1480 Great Wardrobe accounts of Edward IV (1442–83) show the range of silk goods she supplied: sewing silk, silk corses, 'streyte' or narrow ribbon, single and double laces, tassels and buttons of blue silk and gold for garnishing various books, all small luxury items. Between 1483 and 1489 when she dies, she supplied even larger quantities of sewing silk, ribbons and gold fringe, purple lace and gold thread from Venice. She also supplied the decorative tassels and buttons for the coronation gloves and velvet mantles for Richard III (1483–85) and Anne, his Queen. Alice was paid 60s 7d for the white silk and gold lace to tie the Queen's mantle, worn during the coronation vigil procession through the streets of London. She was paid two shillings for her own labour, a very small part of the whole cost. She continued to sell silk items during the early part of Henry VII's reign (1485–1509), including thirty-six buttons of Venice gold at three pennies each and six ounces of red silk ribbon for Henry's coronation robe. These were completed items, not spun or thrown silk to be further worked. This suggests that she was commissioning items from other specialist silk-women, trading and supplying as well as producing silk fashion accessories herself.

Most silk workers in London worked on a more modest scale than Alice and would not have been admitted to the freedom of the city. There were laws that effectively disbarred women from much commercial activity and controlled the amount of credit they could raise. Women could have problems collecting debts owed to them. In her will, Alice left her trusted servant, Thomas Porter, £6 13s.

4d on top of his wages, with the request that he collect the debts owing to her, a task which shows the need any *feme sole* had for at least one responsible male servant, if she was to run her business successfully. It was seen as inappropriate behaviour for a woman to go around and collect money owing to her. It was much better if she was represented by a man.

For most silk-women their work was low paid. Some women did quite well when they found they could turn their domestic skill of spinning wool into the more highly skilled and lucrative art of spinning silk. Other women found work as silk throwsters. Expert sewers made purses or coifs and those with connections to the goldsmith guild learnt to spin the gold around the silk to make the valuable gold thread for braid and embroidery. Nevertheless, many women were very poor and lived from hand to mouth; some did not even own their own spindles or spinning wheels. They paid the agent for the hire of their equipment and he supplied the silk and set the wages, so they never seemed to get out of debt. With these working conditions and the insecurities of city life, they were effectively tied to a master, not free women at all.

With so many women engaged in silk work, it is very surprising that the London silk-women did not form a guild. They were Master craftswomen having completed an apprenticeship, and called themselves the Sylkewymmen and Throwsters of the Crafts and Occupation of Silkewerk, but in contrast to the men, they had no ordinances of their own, no sustained, formal guild structure, made no consistent attempt as a body to keep standards and consequently were never very powerful.

Women did have other options to forming their own silk guild and some joined purely religious guilds and parish fraternities. Alice and her husband Richard were both members of the Penny Brethren of St Lawrence Jewry, and she was also a Sister of the fraternity of the Founders' Company and left it forty shillings for their prayers in her will. Richard was also a member of the Mercers' and Merchant Adventurers' fraternity of St Thomas Becket. Perhaps as a widow, Alice felt more comfortable with the Penny Brethren at her own parish. Membership of a prestigious parish fraternity had status, and could lead one into more elevated social circles, but mostly it was just a safeguard against the demands of business failure and growing old.

Perhaps their relative independence lulled the silk-women into a false sense of security. The successful ones already had an extensive network of friends and colleagues, so probably they did not feel the need for an additional structure. As wives or widows of guildsmen they could call on help at any time, as they did when they were presenting their Petitions to the King. Most wives had limited rights and strong associations with their husbands' guilds and were perfectly satisfied with the religious or social benefits from that.

Perhaps some silk-women were wary of being charged with witchcraft and sorcery, as silk working had long been a 'mistery' craft which was believed to have secret rituals and power. All the other guilds however, had their own secret signs and initiations. A rich tradition of myths and legends grew up among women as they met to spin. Stories from the Gospels of the Distaffs *(Les Evangiles des Quenouilles)*, which connected female work with love and magic were told and retold. A spinning day could be made to foretell the future or a broken thread meant a quarrel. There were old wives' tales that said that the first man to break a thread across a doorway would be your future husband, or that fairies would come and finish the spinning, or be mischievous and tangle the thread. It was even believed, somewhat disingenuously, that it was unlucky to work on Virgin Mary's Day, Saturday.

Silk Spinning in Europe

While the English silk-women did not form a guild, Paris and some other cities, famous for their silk, certainly did. The Paris Book of Trades, *Livre des métiers*, was drawn up and edited by the royal judge, Etienne Boileau in 1270, probably on the orders of King Louis IX (1226–1270). It contains a description of the rights and duties of one hundred Parisian craft guilds, including the five women's guilds, all involved with silk. The tax register, the *Livres de la taille*, of 1292 records eight female silk spinners, and by the next census in 1300 this number had risen to thirty-six journey women, *ouvrieres de soie* (workers in silk), but only one female Master silk cloth producer. It

Les Evangiles des quenouilles, (The Gospels of the Distaff). Women who are friends and business associates get together to spin. French, late 15th century.
Chantilly, Condé Museum.

The Guilds　113

identifies the women who were actually practicing their craft, and notes how women dominated in the silk trades.

Paris had two separate silk spinning guilds. The women who were using large spindles were professionally independent, yet were managed by two male overseers who were commissioners from the town council, *prud' hommes jures*. The small spindle spinners produced the stronger thread and this guild accepted both girls and boys as apprentices for a term of seven years, although in practice it seems only girls and women were members. Despite being a guild of women, men were brought in to oversee the guild along with the senior women.

The silk-spinners were not held in particularly high esteem because they were piece-workers, and like the London women were employed by a silk mistress or agent who owned the expensive raw materials and decided the wages. Worse, the agents often avoided paying the silk workers in cash and offered a substitute or another product, an unsatisfactory arrangement known as the truck system. Spinners were the worst off of all the silk workers and were under-financed and unprotected by powerful husbands. Sometimes the women were accused of cheating and pawning or selling off the good quality silk the agent had given them, and substituting poor quality silk, to make a little profit on the difference. It was a hard and pitiful existence, in sharp contrast to the luxury product they handled.

The silk spinners also had competition from Beguine convents and orphanages. Convents could sell the spun silk cheaply because it had been done *gratis*, to the benefit of their house and the glory of God. An orphanage near Lyon also took advantage of cheap labour by hiring a Dame Lucresse, her name suggesting that she came from the silk city of Lucca, to teach the girls to unwind the silk from the cocoons, prepare thread and wind it onto bobbins. The older girls taught the younger ones and the programme became the next best thing to an apprenticeship for impoverished girls.

Embroidery and Silk Work in Europe

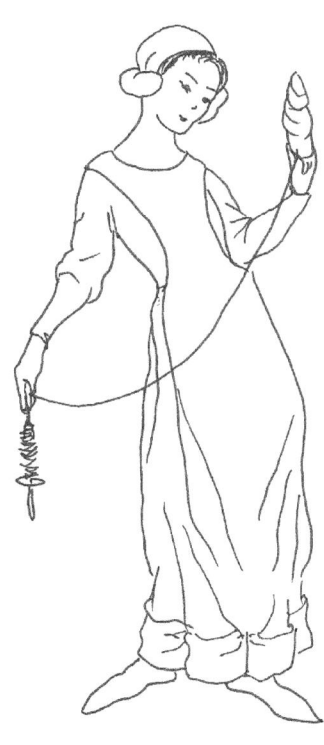

Young girl with a spindle, her long surcote pinned up at the hem, the deeply cut armholes showing her kirtle underneath. Her hair is neatly tucked up into her couvre-chef. Early 14th century.

Jane Shore was the elder daughter of Johan and Ann Lambard, and the mistress of Edward IV. She wears a simple headdress, her hair pulled back and a fitted full-skirted gown.
Brass, by kind permission of the Parochial Church Council of St Nicholas, Hinxworth, Herts.

In 1303 the Provost of Paris, Guillaume de Hangest, approved the earliest known regulations of any embroiderers in Europe, although the guild was not actually registered until 1471. Paris was a sophisticated royal city, geared to offering the rich all the little luxuries of life they so enjoyed. It had a well-developed silk manufacturing trade which flourished until the late fifteenth century, and was almost unique in its attitude, accepting women Mistresses of their own guilds. The silk cap and bonnet makers functioned autonomously with their own *jures*, people nominated to ensure that standards and quality of work were maintained. Their apprenticeship was for seven to eight years and the statutes allowed them to take on one female apprentice as well as family members without requiring the payment of fees. Nevertheless, like the milliners, the husbands took care of the sale of the bonnets and caps, bought the materials and supplied or arranged the capital.

The purse-makers guild, the *faiseuses d'aumendieres sarrazinoises*, made small money pouches and purses for alms. They accepted only girls for an apprenticeship of ten years, which could be reduced to six by payments. In 1299, there were one hundred and twenty-four women, yet this women's guild was supervised by male *jures*, presumably not masters of this craft, who inspected the work for quality and enforced guild ordinances. Only one of the Paris guilds, the weavers of women's headdresses, was actually managed exclusively by the women. In all the other guilds, the women shared the power or played no role at all in governing the guild. This apparent willingness to accept a subordinate role by women in their own guild is surprising, especially in the case of the silk spinners and purse-makers, both exclusively women's guilds.

There were pockets of silk workers in many European countries like Spain and cities and districts, including Strasbourg and Florence. Sericulture had been established in the Po Valley from the tenth century and around Salerno from the eleventh. In Southern Italy, most of the work was done by Jewish, Greek and Arab immigrant families. Lucca was the first centre in Italy for the actual manufacture of silk goods, and was well established by the late twelfth century. There was a guild of women silk weavers in Zurich. They worked for distributors, but on their own account as winders, tackers and warpers in crafts supporting the weaving industry. In Lyon, working silk was a family trade, with the mother and daughters unwinding the cocoons and preparing the thread on the bobbins for the father who was the weaver. Velvet and taffeta weaving was exclusively a male job. If girls had to be hired to unwind the cocoons, as Estienette Leonarde did in 1557, the girls' wages were about half to one third that of the boys and men. One young boy, an apprentice velvet maker from Avignon, earned ten livres per year, *avec bouche, couche et chasse* (with board, room and pants).

The Successful Silk-women of Cologne

The Cologne silk trade was dominated by women from the elite section of society though they did not run it. It was administered by a board, the *Seideamt*, which was founded by statute in 1437. The guilds included the yarn makers – *Garnmacherinnen*, gold spinners – *Goldspinnerinnen*, and the silk makers – *Seideweberinnen*. The silk embroiderers mainly produced heraldic embroideries, liturgical garments, bishops' mitres and ladies' bonnets. Like the other guilds, the silk dyers' charter contained numerous requirements as to quality and raw materials. The silk-women worked very closely together within the guild structure, and this was the basis of a very successful period for Cologne silk in the second half of the fifteenth century. Between 1437 and 1504, one hundred and sixteen silk-women ran their own companies. Records show that in five years, between 1491 and 1495, 100,000 pounds of raw silk was bought and processed by master silk makers in Cologne.

Many silk-women traders and merchants travelled and were active, buying and selling at the Frankfurt Trade Fair and other big fairs. They produced high quality export goods and financed and managed their own deals. Many had their own shops and apprentices, some imported the materials they needed, but most depended on merchants to distribute their silk goods outside Cologne. These were independent women, not employed by the merchants. They had control over their products, set their own prices, and their guild had high standing in the community.

There were some very astute and successful silk families headed by women in Cologne. Tryngen Louback's mother was the silk-maker Niesgin Wyerdt, and her father, Mertyn Neven, was a successful Cologne merchant, silk trader and councillor. Tryngen's husband, Conrad Louback, was also a silk importer. As well as managing her silk business, Tryngen was involved with her husband in the wine trade, and ran his business after his death. She must have been very wealthy, because she purchased about 20,000 pounds of raw silk per annum, about a fifth of the total imported into the city. Her son, Mertyns II Ume Hove, married Lysbeth Lutzenkirchen, and they carried on their parents and parents-in-law's business into the next century.

Lysbeth's mother was Fygen Lutzenkirchen. She was a formidable businesswoman and had been a Master silk-maker since 1474, taking on twenty-five apprentices between 1474 and 1497. Fygen's husband Peter Lutzenkirchen was a major agent for several trading houses and obtained silk from Valencia, supplied gold yarn destined for Genoa and Venice, visited the Brabant Fairs at Bergen

Tailors shop, with stockings on the rail behind the rather unhappy woman customer. Sumptuary laws ensured that at times, only men could make outer clothes, the women were restricted to making petticoats and sewing domestic linen.
Tacuinum Sanitatis 1390 Biblio Nationale, Paris.

op Zoom and Antwerp, as well as the Frankfurt Fair, and was elected to the Senate several times. Both Fygen and Peter served alternately on the guild for eighteen years, but after his death in 1498 she stopped her own silk activities and concentrated on his business. By 1511 Fygen Lutzenkirchen was listed as one of the richest citizens of the city.

It was not easy for all women to make a good living in the textile trades. Some guilds were able to pass very restrictive laws. The town councils of both Cologne and Constance had draconian employment regulations affecting women tailors. They ratified laws in 1426 and again in 1440 with more than a hint of male protectionism. These laws limited the seamstresses to remodelling old petticoats, and prohibited them from making the beautiful and much more prestigious and lucrative silk clothes.

While France was working to produce richly embroidered clothing for the nobility, the English production was mostly for the church. The London Embroiderers were a male guild, established in the fourteenth century. Some of the men are known, like Robert Ascombe who represented the Brouderers with Nicholas Halley in 1370 on the common council of London, and also worked for Richard II in 1394–8. In 1431 John Mounselle was elected mayor, probably the same man who was embroiderer to Henry IV in 1441. The men fought hard to keep out inferior work, especially embroideries sold at the fairs, and in 1423 they petitioned Henry VI to have all unsatisfactory work confiscated or burnt. The embroiderers were feeling threatened and tried to tighten their control over all aspects of their craft, but fashion was changing and it was becoming an age where quicker results were required. Superb, woven brocades were arriving from Italy and Spain, and to the embroiderers' distress, Henry IV (1399–1413) had commissioned vestments not from the embroiderers of London but from the weavers of Florence.

In York between 1394 and 1551 there were eighteen vestment makers, but after the Reformation and the destruction of so many churches, vestments were no longer required. Most makers became Freemen Embroiderers, doing secular work. It was part of a general trend, a further change, and much of the work was now done in commercial premises out of the control of the guilds.

The Transference of Power

By the late fifteenth century the London guildsmen had become most anxious about their prospects and position, especially as there was a down turn in economic conditions. The husbands and other men who had helped promote the various Petitions to the crown to protect the silk-women and their work, had become increasingly involved and had taken over more and more responsibility for the everyday running of the craft. For the women, it must have been easier to let the men who were experienced in the ways of business, control access to the raw materials and production, and sale of the finished goods. The businessmen took the high-profile, high status external role in the craft, as merchants, dealers and financiers, thus acquiring public acclamation and financial rewards. There were mutterings and charges of monopoly and elitism against them, but the guildsmen persisted in promoting laws that protected and favoured themselves, to the detriment of the individual silk-women. It became more difficult for a girl to be an apprentice, for a woman to take her on, or to run her deceased husband's business as a freewoman of London. The latent misogynism, not too far below the surface, led some men to describe the women as inferior, spiritually deficient, undisciplined and disorderly. Women were seen as second class workers and their work as women's work, of little commercial value.

The silk-women do not seem to have protested, not because they could not agitate as they proved with the Petitions, but because in an all-women sphere of work, they did not seem to believe that they had primary rights. They had no ancient customs or guild to back them, legal statutes barred them from political power or influence, they were disbarred from raising significant amounts of finance and were probably reluctant to do anything that would jeopardize the remnants of privilege and status they still had.

Clearly this reluctance to register and defend their own guild, organize their work and take on the male-dominated guild system was devastating, because it left the silk workers vulnerable and unprotected by a formal structure. Opportunities were lost when the women were not publicly seen together as a strong, formally organized and powerful group. There were no women role models with authority and leadership and they did not march in craft parades or wear brilliant and distinctive livery. It seems the women believed that their experience of community and co-operation would be sufficient to safeguard their place at work and in society, but it was not so. By the end of the fifteenth century, the restrictions and controls the male guildsmen had imposed, suffocated the industry to the point of decay. It took the influx of the European silk weavers into England in the late sixteenth century, for the industry to revive and flourish again.

Christine de Pisan 1363–1431 offers Isabeau of Bavaria, Queen of France 1370–1435 a copy of her book of poems. The women wear rich gowns in the fashionable houppelande style and high horned headdresses. The room is furnished with sumptuous silk textiles, wall coverings and bed hangings. 15th century.

MS Harley 4431 British Library.

CHAPTER SEVEN

Silk in Fashion

The story of silk in medieval fashion was, in the end one of availability; access to the finest fabrics and access to the credit to pay for them. It was the merchants, church and the royal court who imported silks and controlled their availability. They had the money, and they set the fashion. Luxurious silken garments were a sign of refinement, prestige and power. Silk and gold captured the imagination, turned heads and incited desire and admiration.

The late Middle Ages, for the men who could afford it, was increasingly a time of flamboyance, clothes in bright colours, richly embellished with as much gold and as many jewels as the garment could stand. It was a time of male display in the court, in the church and in the guilds. Women played a subsidiary role and were often dependent on their men-folk for gifts of fine textiles. People bought at fairs and markets. Some women had their own funds and could spend lavishly on clothes, but few had more than two or three gowns, far less than their men, but then, they often had their jewels.

It was the Age of Chivalry and the Crusades, a time of both exquisite refinement and calculated brutality. The knights attacked and ransacked the palaces and churches of Byzantium and brought back exotic oriental silks as booty and the spoils of war. At home, the fabrics were received with wonder and delight, and they set the fashion for large, complex patterns, using metallic threads and brilliant colours, red, violet, yellow, blue and green.

Our knowledge of costume comes from written descriptions,

criticism of people and their behaviour, Royal Wardrobe accounts, wills, legacies and court records, manuscripts, funereal brasses, sculpture and paintings. Very few actual garments survive, except as fragments. Most clothes just wore out through repeated use and limited cleaning arrangements. Many were turned inside out and re-sewn to hide the stains and wear, or re-cut to fit a child. Finally the remaining bits were used to trim other garments, or made into quilts, mattress covers, aprons and dishcloths. It was common practice when a particularly rich garment wore out, to cut off the gems and burn the item to retrieve the gold. There was also a very lively trade in second-hand clothing; absolutely nothing was wasted.

A few precious tenth and eleventh century fragments of woven silk were found in Milk Street in London, during archaeological excavations in 1976. There were silk ribbons and some fragments of shot silk, with a different colour in the warp and weft. Four of them were tabby weave, one a 2,1 twill, none had been woven in England. Occasionally silk items are found in towns like York and Winchester, but it is only in the tombs of the nobles and church dignitaries that gorgeous, patterned silks are found.

The use of silk for both clothes and furnishing only affected a narrow band of society, because most people only had access to locally grown wool, hemp or linen. Following fashion was an aristocratic pursuit. The ideas gradually filtered down through the general population in a diluted form and influenced the clothing of ordinary people. Clothes could instantly tell others of your occupation, religious values, rank and position in the social scale. As a result of wars, pestilence and plague, society changed and became less influenced by the dictates of the church. Women's costume in particular was controlled by church doctrine and the insistence on the sinfulness of Eve. The church fathers defined appropriate behaviour for women and what they should wear. Women were commanded to cover their hair and conceal their bodies in enveloping mantles and gowns, and were criticized for any extravagance. Some people started to move away from their traditional place in society, to become both physically and socially mobile, to climb the social ladder. It was the fear of not being able to tell who was important that led to a rash of sumptuary legislation, to control what people could or should wear, and when.

Tenth to Twelfth Century

It gives an unbalanced account of a society not to include peasants and villagers, but wearing silk was just not financially possible for them, and there were laws to ensure that people did not try to ape their betters or rise above their station. Peasants' clothes hardly changed in style. They were made of handspun and woven wool, lined with animal skin for warmth. The men wore a short tunic and brais or underpants, under another tunic. The women's chemise or shift was full length and covered by a shorter kirtle and super tunic that was hitched up when she worked. They both wore a mantle or wrap when it was cold and a hood attached to a shoulder cape called a chaperon. Later in the period, some men wore a linen coif that tied under the chin, sometimes with a straw hat over it to protect themselves from the sun. As early as 686, a West Saxon churchman called Adhelm maintained that men and women wore tunics with silk trimmed sleeves, but they would not have been peasants.

By the tenth century most men wore two tunics, the fabric reflecting their social standing. The chainse, or shirt, was made of bleached linen and the bliaut, which came down to the knees, was made of wool or silk. Henry II, Emperor of Germany, was the first to have a very novel addition; a pocket in his white silk damask bliaut. Most people attached their possessions to their belt, but his pocket had a vertical opening just below the neckline, and was hemmed with a wide strip of violet and blue brocaded silk, with green silk piping.

The eleventh century saw few changes in fashion. Women were simply dressed in two or three layers, a long-sleeved chemise of linen or hemp, and over that a simple kirtle and calf length tunic tied with a girdle. When it was cold, she wrapped herself in a cloak or mantle. On her feet she wore sandals or soft low-heeled leather shoes. A noble woman's gown or kirtle might be silk damask or fine wool. It fitted the hips and fell in folds to the ground. Her tunic had narrow sleeves with wide drooping cuffs, edged with embroidery or braid. Maidens wore their hair unbound, while women wore theirs in long swinging plaits, sometimes two or even four, hanging down the front and back. Plaits offered a great opportunity for a little individual style, and could be extended with horsehair, ribbons or little bells that made a tinkling sound as she walked. Sometimes women covered their plaits with long silk casings, called *fouriaux*, or wore a simple jewelled hairband.

Over the short under-tunic, men wore a cote (cotte or coat) which was calf or ankle length. It was cut with magyar or dolman sleeves, decorated with bands of braid around neck and hem and belted low on the hips.

The cote could be worn alone, or covered by a rectangular sleeveless surcoat, known as a tabard. It had originally been worn by the Crusader knights to stop themselves scorching in their armour in the blazing sun, while on campaign. It was split up the back or front, and could be belted or worn loose. For women, the change in fashion in the thirteenth century was from a loose, flowing garment, to one with a closer fit, more 'cut'. Both the tunic and gown were long, the outer garment forming a small train. Her silk or leather belt had a silver buckle and a very long tongue, which swung seductively as she walked. Sometimes she wore a fitted sleeveless super-tunic with long vertical slits for the armholes, and tucked up her skirt to show her pointed shoes. A married woman wore a stylish barbette, a band of linen worn under the chin and over the top of the head, allowing the hair to show. It was held in place by a goffered or fluted linen band or a delicate metal coronet or filet, a style made fashionable by Henry II's wife Eleanor.

Imported Silks

Luxury fabrics were available, but very expensive. Striped tabby silk was popular for linings and secular clothing as well as vestments, furnishings and bed hangings. Velvet was initially used for furnishings and was produced by running an extra warp thread over a series of rods to form a looped pile of silk above a linen tabby base. The pile could be cut, partly cut or left uncut and was known as *cisele* velvet. One of the earliest references to its use in England was in 1278 when Adinettus, Edward I's tailor purchased it in Paris to cover the head of the King's bed, at a cost of 100 shillings. Some velvets had patterns of animals and Kufic or Naskshi script and incorporated metallic thread. The script is not unexpected as many of these beautiful fabrics came from Spain, with its tradition

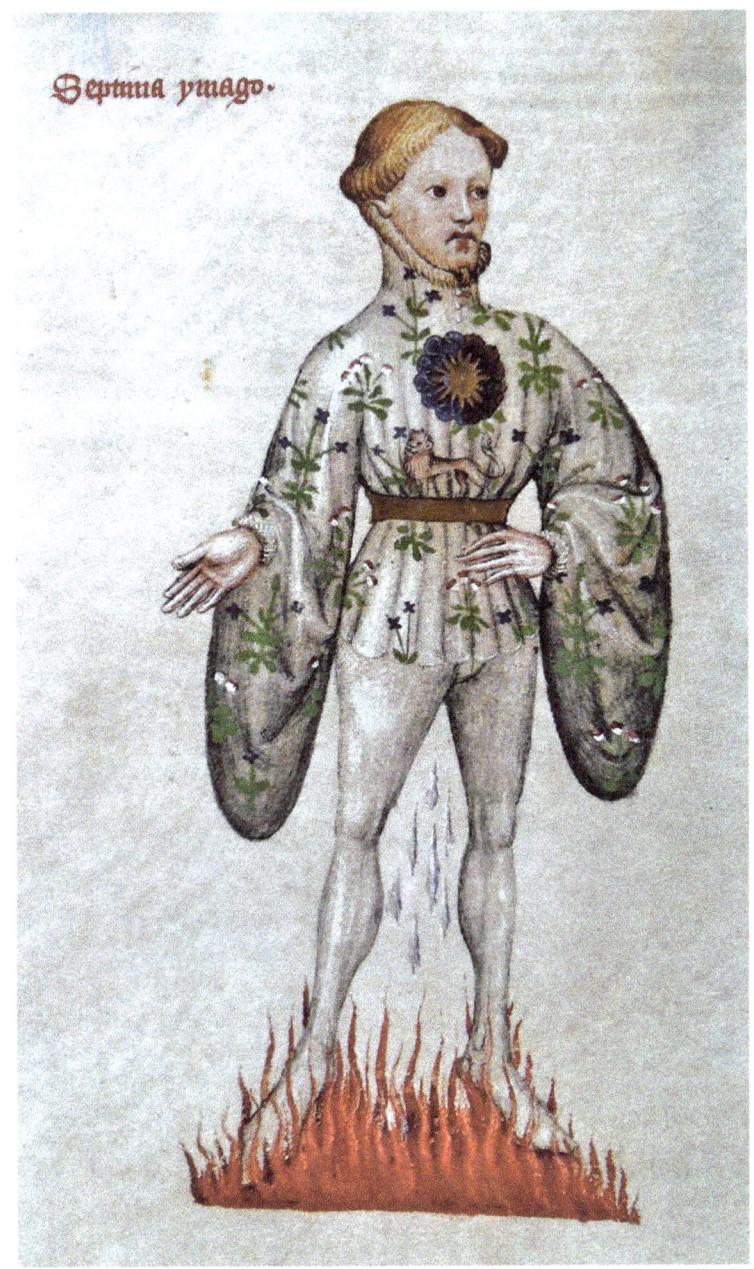

The Sun, adorned in the height of fashion c1408. The young man wears a short, rich silk houppelande with bagpipe sleeves, high neck lined with fur and long fitted hose.

Taken from John Foxton's Liber Cosmographiae, MS Plate 40 fol. 35v Cambridge Trinity College.

of Arabic weavers. Some fabrics were so gorgeous that sumptuary laws were passed so only people of the highest rank could wear them.

The arrival of three envoys from the Mongol Empire to the court of Edward II in 1307 coincided with the re-opening of trade routes to and from the East. The rich silks they brought as gifts for the King inspired a passion for oriental dress. Even William Langland in *Piers Plowman* portrays Charity as preferring 'clean rich robes of cobweb lawn and cloth of Tartary', an early name for China. Twenty-four years later, at a tournament held in Cheapside in 1331, Edward III and his courtiers were dressed in the style of the Tartars. *Pannus de Tars* was presumably a silk cloth from Asia and was recorded in the Great Wardrobe, the King's holding and distribution centre in the East End of London. Lovely striped, mottled and checked velvets, shot through with metallic threads, are also mentioned in the accounts.

A noble woman spinning, wearing a long sleeved chemise and over it a semi-fitted gown, wide cuffs and a long belt wrapped twice around her waist and hips. c1180.

The availability of these expensive silks, plain and patterned lampas weaves, satins and velvets, enabled the nobles and wealthy citizens to rationalize their purchases by maintaining that they were buying them as gifts for the church. They might purchase a silk cloth, *pannus de sirico de auratus*, or a piece of cloth of gold fabric, a *pannus aureus*. Often wills stipulated that the fabric was to be used as a pall, laid over the coffin during the funeral rites and procession for all to admire, before being given to the church to be made up into a vestment. In 1348, a wealthy citizen of Anze, near Lyon wanted his cloth of silk and gold made into a chasuble after his burial. A will of 1310 states: "I desire that a cloth of silk should be bought and that it should be laid over me and I give and bequeath it to the church of St Rambert". These silks were not bought to be worn but were for ostentatious display and a reminder of the donor's generosity, even after death.

In the fourteenth century there are many references to both plain

A King wearing a crimson pile-on-pile velvet robe, a detail from Rogier van der Weyden's St Columba altarpiece, from the Adoration of Magi, 1445 Munich. Many rich silk and gold damasks and velvets had large naturalist patterns featuring fruit, flowers and birds and many velvets were made in Lucca, Genoa and Florence in the 14th century.

and patterned silks. Velvet was still very expensive. In 1329–31, red velvet was 13s 4d per ell (an ell measures about 45 inches), while striped velvet was ten shillings an ell in 1344 and checkered velvet 8s 4d. Lucchese silks are mentioned in the 1388 Inventory of Westminster Abbey. It lists a set made from 'multi-coloured striped cloth of gold from Lucca, inscribed with curious letters' *(panno aureo de Luca varij coloris stragulatum et diveris literis scriptis)*, given to the Abbey by Simon Langham, sometime Archbishop of Canterbury who died in 1376. Satin was widely used for all manner of clothing: doublets, tunics, hanselyns and sloppes, girdles and garters. Blue and green, black, white and red were all fashionable colours in England at the time. Furnishings included cushions and bed-hangings, embroidered in gold or silver gilt, or decorated with painted or stenciled designs that were quicker and cheaper to produce than either embroidery or woven fabric. Chaucer mentions silk and satin, as he paints a picture of luxury and ease in his *Canterbury Tales* (c1387–1400).

I woll gyve him a fether bed
Rayed with golde and ryght well cled
In fyne black sattyn doutremere
And many a pylow and every bere
Of cloth of Raynes to slepe on softe
Hym there not nede to turn ofte

The Cote-hardi

Edward III had a long reign of fifty years, from 1327 to 1377. He was born in 1312 and in 1328 he married Philippa of Hainault. She brought with her, not only numerous courtiers and ladies-in-waiting but also new ideas in fashion, loving support for her husband and a good deal of common sense. It was a more fashion-conscious age and courtiers competed for the latest fashion items and accessories. Philippa was certainly extravagant and loved beautiful clothes and furnishings. She ordered her tailor, William de London, to make a 'robe' of five garments of purple velvet, for her churching ceremonies after the birth of Edward, the Black Prince in 1330. The King's armourer, John of Cologne, was responsible for the embroidery, including the golden squirrels. The whole set or suit of garments needed one hundred and sixty-two ells of fabric, fourteen pounds of gold and sixteen pounds of silk thread. In addition, John needed to purchase extra hooks, cord and thread. The total weight of the garments was daunting and the cost was far more than many people would have earned in a lifetime. Philippa later donated her squirrel robe to Ely Cathedral and it was so vast that between 1321 and 1341 it was cut up and made into three copes for the use of John Crauden, the Prior of Ely.

In 1332 William of London provided Queen Philippa with thirteen matching sets of garments, a total of fifty-five individual pieces plus extra hoods and other items for her to wear at the great feasts, including All Saints and St Mary Magdalene. Her total of seventy-

The Marriage of Melisende Queen of Jerusalem and Fulk of Anjou, 1295. This painting from the late 15thc shows Fulk wearing a fur lined heugue and Melisende court attire of mantle and sideless surcoat. King Baldwin II is wearing a deep fur collar and the clergy are very richly adorned in comparison to Melisende's ladies with their plain shot silk gowns, jeweled cummerbunds and variety of hats.

one garments was less than King Edward's sixty to one hundred new garments each year. He also required gear for jousting and other sports, heraldic flags and banners, tunics and hangings, most of which were supplied by his armourers. They were later responsible for embroidering the Black Prince's jupon, its replica still on display in Canterbury Cathedral.

The most notable fashion change during the fourteenth century was

Silk in Fashion   *131*

the acceptance of the smooth fitting cote-hardi. This garment, with variations, was worn by both men and women after 1330. Its figure-hugging shape extended for men to the knees and then flared out to the floor for women. It needed buttons or lacing down the narrow sleeves and centre front to ensure a good fit. The long flowing bands and streamers attached to the upper arm, known as tippets, became so long they had to be knotted at the end, to stop them from dragging on the floor. The edges were dagged or scalloped, initially a male prerogative, and cut into interesting leafy designs. The heraldic theme continued and the cote-hardi was sometimes parti-coloured, halved or quartered, diagonally striped or rayed into two or more colours. It was all in keeping with the long pointed shoes called poulaine or cracow, named after the city from where they apparently originated. They enraged some members of the church, and Charles V (1337–80) condemned them as a 'deformity, thought up as a mockery of God and His Holy Church'.

Wealthy women paraded in their silk damask cote-hardi. It was flared and gored and probably cut on the bias. Its smooth fit over the bust and hips leant itself to the swaying walk that was universally admired. Sometimes it had little slits in the front, called fitchets, so the lady could get at her embroidered silk alms purse hanging on the belt around the waist of her undergown, where it was protected from 'cut-purses' and other vagabonds who might steal it. The super-tunic of the 1350s had deep curved armholes, edged with fur. This graceful style allowed the kirtle or cote-hardi to be seen underneath, and the lovely silk girdle worn on the hips. An especially rich and beautiful girdle might be a gift from a husband or lover. One writer advised that the fur trim should be removed in the summer months, because it attracted fleas. In fact a little furred flea band was sometimes worn on the wrist for just that purpose.

Necklines got lower and wider, exposing bare shoulders. Older women wore a fine linen wimple, draped under the chin, covering the neck and tucked into the scooped neckline, and topped by a shoulder-length veil, fluted at the edge. Plaited hair was now looped up at sides of the face in front of the ears, and covered with a net or crespine. Chaperons continued to be worn outdoors by both men and women, with the long liripipe tail hanging down the back. By the end of the fourteenth century the noblewoman's hair was

Knight bidding his lady farewell, depicted on a gilded wooden parade shield. She is wearing a very rich, fur trimmed velvet gown with a tall hennin headdress. The text says 'You or Death' but with a skeleton included, the prognosis is not very good.
British Museum.

completely hidden by an increasingly important headdress, with a jewelled and embroidered caul, over which was attached an ornamental padded roll. Children in manuscript illustrations seem to wear chaperons, tunics and hoods, plainer replicas of their parents' clothes.

All this emphasis on the appearance of the clothing didn't hide the fact that people and their clothes must have smelt dreadful. In the fourteenth century not everyone washed, but they did use many scents and perfumes. Violet was most popular. Pomanders were made and a primitive atomizer, called a 'cyprus oyslet', sprinkled scented powder when it was squeezed.

'Hungarian water' was the first perfume with an alcohol base. It contained cedar, rosemary and turpentine and was given to Charles V in 1370. Smart women used creams and ointments, powders and toothpaste and dyed their hair blond or black, but never red which symbolized wickedness.

In the 1360s men were wearing an embarrassingly short, hip-length garment called the paltok, with their hose attached to the sides by laces with little metal tips, called points. The moralists were outraged, and blamed it on the foreigners, especially the fashionable Hainaulters who had arrived with Queen Philippa. Under the paltok, men wore a gibbon, also known as a pourpoint, jupon or jerkin, next to the shirt. It was tightly fitted and hooked at the sides, and was popular in its many variations, for over 100 years. It evolved from the gambeson, a thick, fur-lined or quilted garment worn to stop the armour from chaffing. By the second half of the fourteenth century it had become the doublet, with its two quilted layers. Ladies and hired needlewomen spent hours

Silk in Fashion *133*

decorating surcoats, robes and mantles with heraldic devices. Style was everything. Sir John Chandos must have looked amazing as he took to the battlefield in 1370 under the command of the Black Prince. He might have escaped death, except he got tangled up in the folds of his lavish trailing embroidered robes.

After the French king, known as John the Good, died in 1364, men started to wear black as a sign of mourning and this convention continued, becoming even more severe for royal women. Eleanor of Pointiers, a court lady in the reign of Philip the Good, maintained that the Queen of France had to remain in her black-hung bedroom for a year, but less was demanded of other members of the court. The custom of wearing black probably came from Spain, but was not then a universally accepted colour for mourning. The Egyptians chose yellow, an allusion to withered leaves, the Ethiopians gray, a reminder of ashes, while white signified purity. After the period of mourning, deep violet could be worn, being a mixture of the red of royalty, and the blue of sorrow and trust in Heaven.

Of all the Kings of England, Richard II who reigned for twenty-two years from 1377 to 1399, was the most devoted to fashion and the butt of much criticism for his extravagance. Silk lampas and baldekyne were superseded by the fashionable satins and damasks and he just had to be the first to have a black silk damask doublet. He adored velvet, and for his marriage to his second wife Isabella in 1396, he accumulated a splendid collection of figured velvets. They included polychrome or *mottele attabys*, voided velvet on a satin ground, *pannes ici*, damask figured velvet, sometimes with gold, and even *velvet velut*, an early reference to pile on pile velvet. He had one coat that was valued at 30,000 marks, and a long robe of green damask, made for his appearance in court in 1393–4. His uncle Thomas, Duke of Gloucester, also owned a gown and coat, (cloke) of black silk damask at the time of his disgrace in 1397. The dark coloured silks became a 'must have' fashion, but eventually Edward IV (1461–1483) limited its wear to people over the degree of knight, an edict clearly ignored by the people.

The Houppelande

By 1380 the cote-hardi was losing favour and men started to wear the houppelande, lined with fur for the winter. It was a full, loose, outer garment, flaring out from the padded shoulders, the first sign of the bulky look that would become such a distinctive feature in the Tudor age. The houppelande was full length but it got shorter over the next few decades, especially for the young and trendy. It had very full sleeves with a wide cuff. Soon an alternative, the bag sleeve, buttoned at the wrist became very popular because it could be a useful pocket or pouch. The neckline rose almost to the ears and was edged with fur. Its most distinctive feature was the pleats that formed at the waist when it was belted. Initially the belt was placed at the natural waistline, but soon the fashion-conscious man wore his belt very low, on the hip. Over his shoulder he slung a hat, on a long ribbon. It was called a *chapeau bra* and was never intended to be actually worn on the head. Hose were often parti-coloured, one red and one green, cut on the cross. They had a seam up the back to improve the fit and were attached by points to the paltok. With them they wore long pointed shoes.

Mastercraftsman or Guildsman, wearing a close-fitting cote-hardi with a low decorated belt, a mantle around his shoulders and leather soles on his fitted hose, mid 14th century.

This lady is wearing a pelisson over her tight sleeved and buttoned surcoat and kirtle. The couvre-chef and wimple indicate she is a married woman.

Silk in Fashion

For some time, women had been wearing a vast circular floor-length cloak called a pelican or pelisson. It did not have defined sleeves, but otherwise was similar to the houppelande. The men's houppelande often opened down the front, but the women's was pulled on over the head. The houppelande was a very graceful garment, warm and comfortable, the distinctive radiating pleats held in place by a decorative belt placed just under the bust. The deep flowing sleeves could be a bit tricky to manage so it sometimes had decorated slits in the upper part of the sleeves for the arms to come through. These fitchets were edged with fur or braid, just like the old pelisson cloak.

The high necks and collars required the hair to be drawn well off the face, and tucked under a headdress. Richard II's first wife, Anne of Bohemia, is credited with introducing some of the most extraordinary headpieces. By now the ear cauls or silk net crespines had crept higher, forming two little horns that would get progressively larger and wider. Some headdresses had a padded circular roll of fabric called a *bourrelet*, which gradually rose higher into a horseshoe shape, with a fitted decorated undercap underneath. Some had silk or linen veils, fluted and piled up and attached to wires or an under-prop. The men's hood changed shape, and instead of being worn like a balaclava, the whole chaperon was lifted up on top of the head. Sometimes the liripipe was flung nonchalantly over the shoulder, or pinned onto the costume, but more often the tail was wound around the chaperon on the head, holding it all in place and allowing the fancy dagged edges to show to advantage. Men of fashion soon got tired of doing this every time they put it on, so the tailor stitched it into place in the most flattering and becoming style adding feathers, fringes or garlands to give height and importance. To really put a price on your head, the feathers had to be ostrich, and they could be as valuable as the rest of the garments together.

Fifteenth Century Fashions

The early fifteenth century began with the reign of Henry IV, (1399–1413). He was married to Mary Bohun in 1395 and later to Joan of Navarre. He was very sensitive about his right to kingship and cautious about spending too extravagantly or asking parliament for money. To keep down the cost on his cloth of gold or velvet, he sometimes had the weft made of yellow silk. The long enveloping fur-lined heugue became popular, possibly as an antidote to the short tunics and houppelandes, which rose higher and higher. The hose also crept upward over the thighs until eventually, in a stroke of genius they were joined together as tights and combined with the breeches. Some hose were soled with soft leather, and wooden pattens or clogs were worn over them in wet weather.

The whole silhouette for women was tall and willowy and by the mid-fifteenth century had reached its apogee. The long trained gowns, with the high, tight belt, decorated with jewels for special occasions, drew attention to the tiny bust. The neckline of the gown became wider, forming a deep V in the centre front and the outer edges rolled over to form a collar making a splendid area for the display of beautiful jewellery. The wide sleeves got longer and trailed on the ground, while the silk damask undergown's tight sleeves covered the knuckles. Headdresses came in a wide variety of shapes: turbans, truncated flower pots, horned, triangular, fluted, or suspended on wires like fluttering butterflies. The hennin or steeple headdress caused a sensation with its long diaphanous silk veil that allowed the beautiful silk damask cone to show through. It was fashionable at the Burgundian court, though less often seen in England. Most headdresses had a little velvet loop in the centre front, to help adjust and pull the headdress into place. They all had one thing in common: not a single hair was permitted to show. The high smooth forehead gave the high-browed look and any offending hair had to be plucked out.

Not everyone was the fashionable shape and women started wearing a short-sleeved corselet, laced in front with a wire belt to tighten the waist and push up the bust. Some women inserted little pads into their chemise to improve the bustline and a pad was placed on the stomach under the gown to give the stylish full rounded line, a fashion credited to Isabeau of Bavaria who was rather plump. Her shape just wasn't right for the current look, and she went to endless trouble, taking baths in asses' milk, sweating for hours in steam rooms, having the physician place cupping glasses all over her body, all in the pursuit of fashion. Naturally she had a whole range of cosmetics at hand, made up of crocodile glands, boars' brains and wolves' blood, combined with strange oils.

As the women's clothes got longer and more extravagant, the men's got shorter and shorter, the doublets were boned and stiffened. By now the long-toed shoes had become absurd, and rumour has it that the points had to be stuffed with tow or moss or held up by a little chain attached to a band under the knee. It was all rather extreme. Then quite suddenly the fashion for the high headdress was over. The hennin was shortened and set at the back of the head, still with its velvet loop but now with a small transparent silk veil, folded in the centre to give a heart shape. A black gauze hood with a veil was introduced, which fell onto the shoulders and later developed into the French hood of the sixteenth century. Collars got flatter and spread out on the shoulders away from the V-shaped neck. The wide sleeves were slashed to show the rich brocaded undersleeve, or the fine pleated lawn chemise. It is said that slashing the fabric started in Germany, but by 1450 it had spread to France and England. The *Roman de la Rose* mentions 'sewn in sleeves', a reference to the practice of varying the costume by having extra sets of sleeves, made of rich fabric and laced onto the garment. The *surcotes ouvertes* or front-opening women's gown heralded a further change. The stiffened farthingale or 'keep thy virtue' was initially a highly decorated V-shaped section of petticoat, starched and covered with taffeta. It was said to have been invented in 1470 by the wife of King Henry V of Portugal, who tried to hide her illicit pregnancy from her impotent husband. Some gowns had a decorative hem that could be replaced when it got worn or irretrievably dirty. The whole shape of women's dress was changing, becoming wider on the shoulders, and more cone-shaped and structured in the skirt, with wide split sleeves gathered into the wrist with voluminous outer sleeves, and lacy frills. Some immense over-sleeves were turned back and edged with fur — a last reminder of the Middle Ages and heralding the bulky square look of the Tudor period.

Marriage King Philip III to Marie of Brabant 1274. Both are wearing rich mantles embossed with the fleur-de-lys of France. Marie's fur-trimmed sideless surcoat is worn over a pink kirtle. The smart young man behind Philip wears a dagged tabard and two-coloured parti-hose with long pointed poulaine shoes.

Silk in Fashion

Waterfall Jacket, handspun, dyed and hand knitted silk. Photo taken in the Waikuku Lavender Gardens, North Canterbury by Bill Wilson.

CHAPTER EIGHT

Spinning Silk

Silk is a joy and a delight, and working with it can change your life. There are a many different styles of silk fibre and ways to spin it, so choose the kind of silk and the best method to produce the perfect thread for the current project, be it weaving, knitting, embroidery, braid making or lace.

There is no wrong way to spin silk, but most problems arise from thinking that all silks are the same, and that there is only one way to spin it; into a long smooth glossy thread, as finely as possible. Some silks, like top quality Bombyx mori and tussah silk can be spun this way, but many of the other styles have short fibres, are knotty, chalky in colour or sticky to handle. These will never spin into a smooth lustrous fibre but they make wonderful novelty yarns with interesting textures. Many people learn to spin wool first, where the finest, thinnest yarn is the most highly esteemed, but silk is silk, not wool and should be handled differently. If silk is spun very finely, it will look and feel like string. It will drop when it is knitted and loose its sparkle and lustrous feel, the very things that make silk special.

Of all the natural fibres, wool has the most bounce and cotton the greatest capacity to sag and drop. Silk is in the middle and has some elasticity, so the main object is to spin the silk fibre around air to incorporate as much lift as possible and highlight the lustre. This is done by first spinning the silk tops or sliver quite softly to incorporate the most air and then plying it more firmly to make a soft rounded yarn. If the reverse is done, with a tightly spun and loosely plied yarn, the result is a hard, dull thread with the life squeezed out of it, and a flat sloppy plied yarn that will feel stringy and not wear well.

Preparing your wheel

Silk is very light and if you have been using your wheel for greasy wool, you will need to clean all the moving parts before you oil it, to make it run smoothly and to ensure that the silk remains clean and does not pick up old fibres or grease.

Oil your wheel in a logical way so no part is missed, across the top, then the middle section, and finally across the bottom. Put the tiniest drop of oil on the leathers, around the pin and orifice, and on either side of the bobbin. Now apply a drop of oil to each point across the middle section of your wheel, including the centre hole, and finally around the foot peddles. Sit comfortably, and quietly treadle using both feet. Establish a gentle continuous rhythm, to distribute the oil evenly.

All wheels will accommodate two feet, even if the treadle is very small. Lucky you if you have a double treadle! Try this experiment: treadle using one foot, and feel the angle of your back. It will twist and sag lower on one side. If you doubt this, sit in front of a mirror. Now place two feet on the treadle, and note how you are sitting more squarely on the chair and your back has become balanced. If you want to spin for hours at a time and your back to last in good condition until the end of your life, you must learn to treadle with two feet. It will feel a bit odd to begin with, but persevere. Once you feel that sense of balance, you will be pleased to have made the change.

Young spinner, her overtunic tucked up like an apron. After a drawing by Jean Fouquet, probably before 1460.

Spinning Silk

There are many different styles and forms of silk suitable for spinning, but the two most readily available are the domesticated white Bombyx mori and the wild, honey-coloured tussah. They both come in a myriad of different grades. Start with A1 grade in a silk brick, tops or sliver, the best you can find. Do not think that silk, because it's called silk, will do. Poor quality silk will never spin into a beautiful, smooth, lustrous thread.

First check the quality and length of the staple because that will determine the way you spin it. Carefully tear off about 20cm or 8 inches of silk fibre. Grasp one end of the silk and fold the fingers over it, against the palm of your hand, to anchor it. Use your other hand like a gentle clamp and place your thumb and the first finger about 5 cm or 2 inches lower. Give the silk fibres a little tug upwards and hear them make a snapping sound. Keep moving the bottom hand down the silk, a little at a time until the fibres start to part. Notice the gloss, and the way good quality silk will have all the fibres lying parallel and open, free of knots, noils and tangles. Note its staple length. Good spinning silk should be between 10–15 cm, ie 4–6 inches long. If the silk is very short in the staple, matted, dull or a poor colour, set it aside for another project and find some better quality silk. There are other methods for spinning short staple silk; nothing is wasted.

Now take the primary thread on your bobbin, and pass it through the front orifice on your wheel. Hold it firmly in either hand, whichever one is right for you. Turn the wheel clockwise and gently start treadling. Use the thumb and first finger to pinch and slide down the primary thread, controlling the position of the twist.

Now take a 20 cm portion of silk tops or sliver and while you treadle slowly, flick the furry ends underneath the primary thread between the oriface and your fingers so that the silk fibres are gathered in by the twisting primary thread. Keep the thumb and first finger of the front hand always on the thread, controlling the position of the twist, as you gently slide them down the silk, smoothing it as you go. On no account let the silk get under your fingers and into the loose fibre, because you will never be able to open it out to spin into a thread.

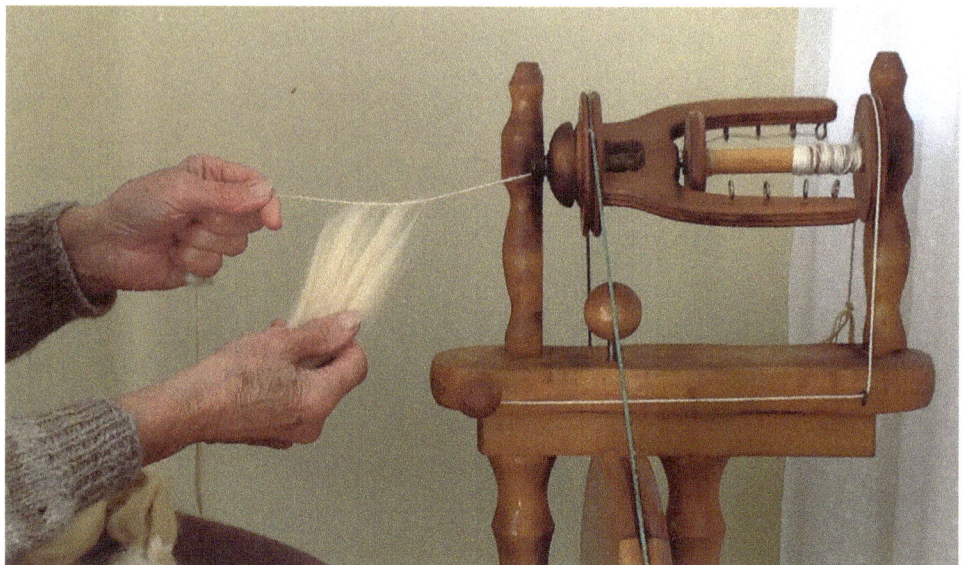

Joining in the furry ends, suitable for both Bombyx mori and Tussah silk.

The back hand has an equally important but different job to do. It must prepare the silk to be spun by fanning it out over the palm of your front hand. The fibres make a wide V, and it is easy to glance down and check that all the fibres are lying smoothly and are incorporating as much air as possible. That is the secret: the back hand must keep preparing the silk by fanning it out.

The two most important things are:

- The front hand must squeeze and slide down the fibre controlling the position of the twist, and smoothing the thread, never jumping on and off, unless you want lumps and slubs.

- The back hand must prepare the silk fibre, opening it by fanning it out, and working in rhythm to let the spun silk gather onto the bobbin.

Do not be tempted to dampen your fingers to help twist the threads, or even apply hand cream before you spin. Use hand cream some time before you start spinning, not just as you start. Give it time to be absorbed into your skin. Silk picks up every little bit of grease, dust or perspiration and although you will not see it at the time,

Fanning out the silk, working it over the palm of the hand.

when the yarn has been woven or knitted there will be a long grey line across your work, and you will not be able to get the stain out or even over-dye it. It is permanent.

Things to check

The tension on your wheel should be balanced, neither so tight that it grabs and drags the spun fibre onto the bobbin, nor so loose that the thread sags and is not taken up. The wheel must play its part, and draw the thread smoothly and firmly onto the bobbin. If the thread dips as it goes towards the orifice, tighten the tension a little, turning the break-band knob a fraction at a time, just one click, that is all. Keep adjusting the tension, click by click until the balance feels right and you can feel the wheel drawing the silk smoothly onto the bobbin.

Some silk, especially tussah, may 'fly' when you start opening it up and spinning it. Try folding the length of sliver in half, so there

Spinning Silk

Sit back in a relaxed position and keep your hands a good distance apart as you fan out the silk.

is a smooth loop of silk at the bottom, and double the amount of fluffy ends to join in. This smooth loop is much less liable to break up and 'fly' as it rubs against your knees. If the fibre gets matted and muddled in your hands, try folding it over the first finger and spinning from the fold.

Check the height of your chair to ensure that it is neither too high nor too low, and sit well back in a relaxed position. If you crouch over your work, your back will ache. This is a smooth long draw system, and your nose does not have to be involved. Consciously relax your hands to ensure a soft spin. Good quality silk has a long fibre and won't escape, so there is no need to grip it tightly. This is gentle, relaxed spinning so keep your hands a good distance apart to lengthen the draw, and let the wheel do most of the work. The longer and smoother the draw, the more even the twist and the faster the silk will be spun onto the bobbin.

When you sit at your wheel, you are part of a harmonious circle that joins your feet with your back, your heart, head, hands, the silk and the wheel. Spinning sets up its own rhythm. If you are peddling quietly, then your thoughts and hands will move together, your heart rate will slow down and you will have a real sense of wellbeing, a time out, a real bonus in a busy life. You can read while you spin or choose some nice music, classical or modern but perhaps not the William Tell overture, which could have you galloping along! The silk will work its own magic and a feeling of contentment, harmony and balance will result.

If silk spinning is new to you, undoubtedly the hardest part will be to make the thread thick and even enough to knit, crochet, or for a weft for weaving. You may want your silk to be very thin and tight for a warp or lacemaking. The important thing is that by sitting back, and working it over the palm of your hand, you determine exactly the character of the yarn for your project. So, start spinning and see how it goes. Every so often, double the spun thread back on itself to gauge the way it will look and feel once it is plied. By all means continue to spin it very finely, but then knit some, and see if you like the result. Silk needs to be knitted on needles at least two sizes smaller than the pattern says for wool or acrylic. If you are happy using size 2 mm needles, then that is just fine. If you want to use commercial patterns, your silk needs to be comparable to a four-ply or double knitting yarn. Spinning silk is different from wool, and it is much harder to make it soft, thick and even, but persevere. In the end the results are well worth it.

Try this experiment. Start with the first hook on your flyer and spin that. When you change to the next hook, consciously try to spin the next section a little thicker, and so on, as you move over the hooks. Do the same with the next bobbin, so that when you come to ply it, you can actually see and feel the difference. You can choose to spin the thickness you want. It is all to do with training your hands and eyes. An expert is not the person who can spin the finest thread but the one who can spin a whole range of silks using different methods to produce specific and beautiful results. If you are wanting a very long smooth even fibre say for a warp or embroidery, there is an argument for buying it ready spun, on a cop or in a hank, and then spinning a more interesting and individual thread with more character for the weft or embellishment. Try to spin yarn in ways that the manufacturer cannot. Then your work will be fresh and unique, a reflection of your individuality and talent.

Gold Jacket, hand spun and knitted silk, with additional gold metallic yarns and gold bead embellishment down the front and high at the centre back.

Plying Silk

With plying, if your wheel allows it, use a smaller size whorl to put more twist in the thread and improve the ratio. Place both full bobbins near one another, and if possible, put your lazy kate slightly behind your chair. This will enable you to have a nice long draw, and the two threads to be parallel and at the same tension. If it is hard to get a long draw because your bobbins are on pins on the wheel itself, try threading the bobbins onto two knitting needles in a shoe box.

The trick with plying silk is to ensure that both threads keep an equal tension and one thread is not joining in at a looser tension or worse, wrapping itself around the other thread. This uneven tension may not be obvious at first, but when you come to knit it, the garment will have a diagonal pull, the stitches all marching resolutely off to one side. Knitting a little sample will reveal this straight away. Unfortunately this yarn will not come right, even after washing, stretching, weighting or blocking so set it aside for using with other fancy yarns.

Back to plying: attach your two threads to the primary thread on the bobbin. There are lots of methods, but a reef knot (right over left and under, left over right and under) is an excellent choice because it will just pull apart smoothly when you are finished. Place the fingers of your front hand between the threads to control each separately, and pinch them to control the twist.

Place the fingers of your other hand well behind you, separating the threads and pinching and controlling them. Peddle, turning the wheel in the opposite direction, probably anti-clockwise if you have spun your silk clockwise in the first instance. Now check the tension on your wheel. You will probably have to tighten it a bit. Continue in a smooth rhythm until all the silk has been plied. Try counting, "one-two-let it on", to establish an easy rhythm with a regular number of treadles and twists.

Washing Silk

The plied silk needs to be skeined and washed to relax it and set the twist. This step is essential with silk, as unwashed silk can drop up to 10 cm over the length of a knitted garment. Loosely tie the skeins in four places and then fill a bowl with hand-hot water. Add your usual hand-washing liquid, a silk wash like Tenestar, or even a good quality dishwashing liquid with a neutral Ph rating. Avoid soap powder. If the powder does not dissolve completely it will leave specks on the silk, and most machine washing powders are too harsh and have additives and whiteners to bleach and remove difficult stains and are not suitable for silk.

Slosh the skeins gently so they get completely wet, but do not leave them to soak. Squeeze the water out and refill the bowl with water of the same or slightly cooler temperature, to rinse the silk completely. Refill the bowl once more with warm water. You may wish to use a little water softener or fabric conditioner in the final rinse. Squeeze the water out of the skeins and roll them in a towel and stamp on them. If you have a number of skeins, then put them in a wash bag and spin the water out using the final 'spin only' setting on your washing machine. It is important to get the water out as quickly as possible, so never drip dry silk. It will dry stretched, hard and dull.

The skeins of silk will look just awful, flat and nasty, but do not despair. Give each skein a really good shake and hang it on an airing frame, or on the line but not in the bright sun. Every time you go past, give it a shake, to allow the air back into the fibres and to break them up so they don't cling together looking flat and miserable. Finally, when the skeins are almost dry, you can put them in the tumble-dryer for a few minutes to fluff them up, or give them a really good beating by flicking them against the back of a chair and snapping them between your hands. An excellent exercise for a bad day. Silk is tough and strong, and will come up smiling. You are in charge, so don't be afraid of it.

Different styles of silks

Silk comes in lots of different forms as well as bricks, slivers and tops. All spinning silks are 'waste silk'. This is rather a misnomer as all silks are useful. 'Waste silk' refers to all the different styles of silk fibre except filament silk, the continuous thread that has been wound off the cocoon and used by the manufacturer.

Most styles of silk come in both Bombyx mori and various shades of tussah, as well as being bleached, carded or combed. Some you might find are:

- **Silk bricks, both Bombyx mori and Tussah**
- **Carded, combed silks**
- **Floss, Blaze and Cocoon strippings**
- **Bleached, carded or uncarded silk noils**
- **Degummed cocoons**
- **Mawata caps and handkerchiefs**
- **Throwsters silk**
- **Laps and batts**
- **Gummy silk**
- **Carrier rod waste**

Stripy silk jacket, handspun and dyed in a continuous way so that the silk knits up into stripes and fairisle, finished at the bottom with a pleated edge.

The biggest mistake is to try to spin them all into a long, smooth, glossy thread. They are not designed for that. You choose the method of spinning to match the fibre, to produce a particular result. All silk is imported, mostly from China and the different forms of silk are not always available. If you find a special one, get enough to complete your project.

Silk Bricks. These are made up of thick, untwisted ropes of silk fibres, carded and finely combed, about 3 metres long and weighing between 125 and 150 gms. Each is wound into a brick shape and usually packed into lots of sixteen bricks, about two kilograms in total weight. The bricks can vary considerably in quality. The best is A1. These are fully carded and finely combed, bright and glossy, with fine even fibres around 10–15cm (4–6 inches) in length, free of knots and rubbish. Choose a long smooth spinning method for a glorious, lustrous, top quality yarn. Lesser quality bricks can be duller and more chalky, more matted in texture, carded but not combed, with a staple length of as little as 2cm, (1 inch), so be warned! Always check the staple length, or ask for a sample before you buy.

Carded and combed silks. These are mixed length fibres that have been carded and/or combed, and are usually sold as sliver or tops. They come in various qualities so do check the fibre length before buying. They can spin up into a smooth yarn, but are usually less lustrous or more chalky and may not be A1 quality. Some are described as cut silk, and some have a very short staple. Both these sorts will spin into a wonderful, soft slubby yarn. This could be a good silk to hand card with other fibres, and it is the usual way of presenting mixed fibres, silk carded with wool, alpaca, cotton etc.

Blaze, Floss and Cocoons strippings are the broken fibres from the outside of the cocoon and the last weak fibres inside the cocoon, before and after the filament thread has been reeled off. They come in a variety of natural colours from white to dark brown, including a super egg-yoke yellow. The yellow is in the sericin gum, and will wash out eventually with repeated hot washings. The fibre has a matt finish and the texture is more like cottonwool. Blaze is the loose silk that the silkworm has spun to attach itself to the twigs or frame before starting to spin its actual cocoon. Silk floss has traditionally been used for embroidery. Partly degummed cocoon strippings can be used in felt and paper making and they are easy to spin. If the staple length is short, or very mixed then use a woollen spin, guiding the fibres through evenly. Experiment with the tension, until you

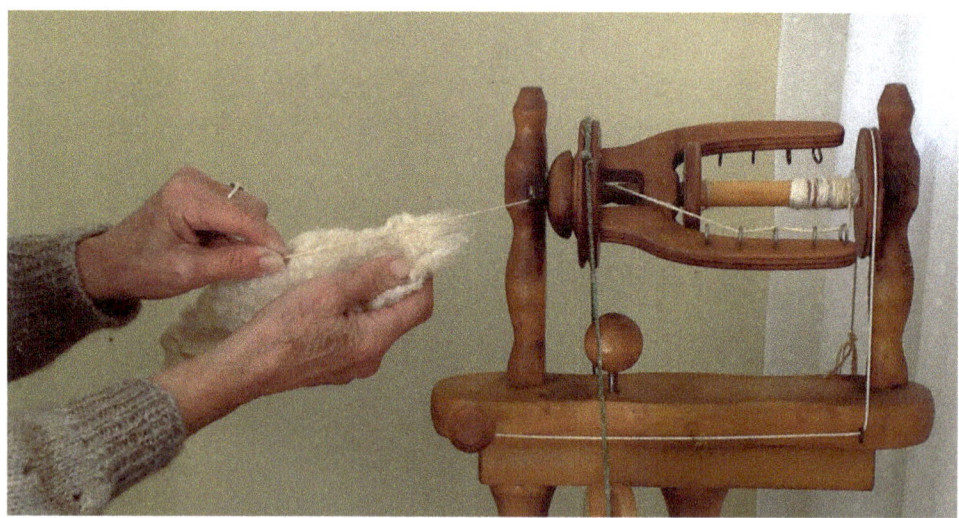

Laying the primary thread over the cocoon strippings, noil or throwsters silk so the short ends will twist in together.

get the wheel doing half the work of drawing out the strippings and then springing the spun thread onto the bobbin. It's a balancing act.

Noil, uncarded, carded and bleached. Noil has great possibilities. It has the shortest fibre length of all the waste silks and some are little better than floor sweepings. Noils are the little knots and knops, the residue left after the silk has been repeatedly carded, combed and the best silk removed. The fibres often contain little bits of rubbish, which show up as black flecks. Noil has little gloss, but takes the dye very well and makes an interesting textured, high twist yarn. Carded noil can come as fragile sheets with a pleated effect, the result of going through the carding machine. Try rolling small sections into a soft cylinder and holding it inside your back hand. Lay the primary thread through the middle of it, and let the twist come right down and inside the cylinder of silk, gathering the very short fibres into itself. This can be done with one-hand only, or use the top/front hand to pinch and release to control the amount of twist, and ease out any thicker parts that form in the thread. This high twist, low luster yarn dyes beautifully, and is excellent for giving texture to weaving or for plying with more slippery silks.

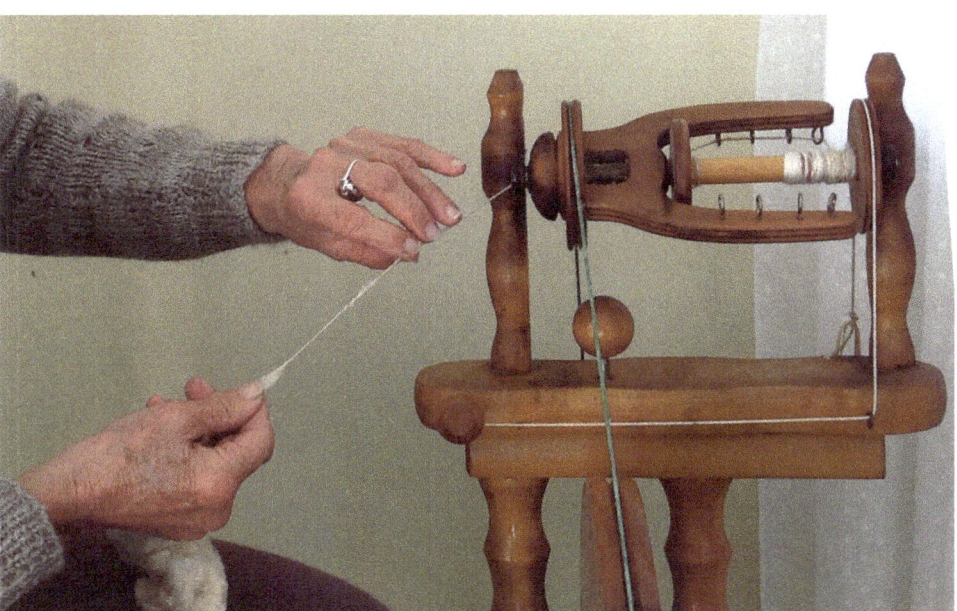

Pinch and relax the front hand to release the twist into the short silk fibre, while drawing the back hand further and further back.

Degummed Cocoons. This is the innermost part of the cocoon, after the pupa has been extracted. The fibres have been washed and dried to remove the gum. They are of mixed length, some are very long indeed and are mixed in with the mass of little bobbles. You could tease them out and spin the silk as usual, but why would you, when it is already in fantastic bobbles. Tighten the tension a little on your wheel and tear off a handful of the degummed cocoons. It is not necessary to open it all out. Use its intrinsic character, and let the bobbles spin through, like beads on a string. This silk has a wonderful texture and looks fantastic when incorporated into a woven piece, or as part of a fancy pattern in a knitted garment or couched down in embroidery.

Mawata Caps and Handkerchiefs. Mawata is made from the broken cocoons after the silkmoth has emerged. The cocoons now have a hole at one end, so it is no longer possible to unwind it as a continuous filament. The cocoons are placed in hot water to dissolve the sericin or silk gum and then between 8 and 15 cocoons are stretched over a porcelain or metal hoop frame, one layer on top of another, to form a 'cap'. A bundle of around thirty caps is called a 'bell.'

There is a 'Proper Way' and an 'Easy Way' to deal with mawata. The Proper Way is to punch a hole through the cap, and stretch it into an even larger circle, which gets thinner and longer until it eventually breaks forming a long length. This is then teased out further and further until a long fluffy sausage is formed on the floor. This is slow and tiring because it is sticky and tough. It is hard on your hands, your shoulders, and difficult to spin and control the thickness.

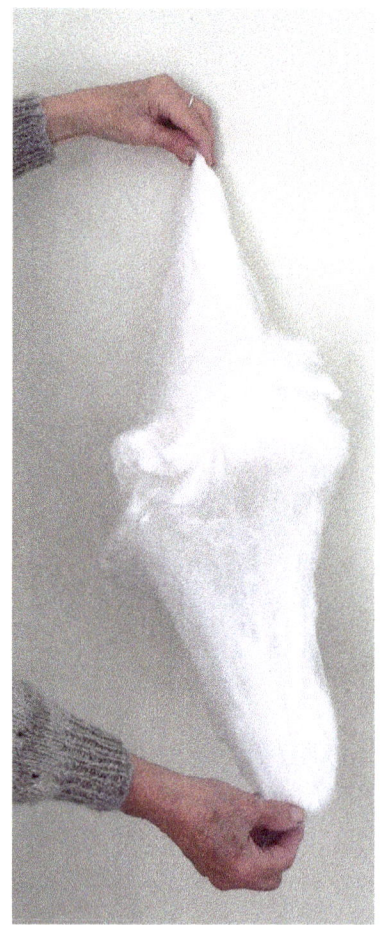

Separating a Mawata cap by gripping the bulk from the inside and one layer on the outside and giving it a sharp pull.

There is an Easy Way to deal with mawata caps. Put one hand right up inside the cap and grab hold of almost all the other layers, except the top one, which you pinch with your outside hand. With a quick snap, pull your hands apart and one complete layer comes off. Even better it is already in a large V shape, allowing plenty of air around the fibres so they do not stick together. It requires no further preparation and it is ready to spin on your wheel, spindle or to thigh roll. It is quick and easy and not tiring at all. With the handkerchiefs, just peal off one layer at a time. Both caps and handkerchiefs dye beautifully and as the colour goes right through, the rainbow effects can be magical. Clean and dried mawata caps are stretched out evenly by four people and laid one on top of another to make a silk duvet.

Throwsters silk is the waste from the twisting and throwing machines and sometimes the silk thrums, the warp waste cut off the loom. Throwsters can be spun into an exciting imitation boucle. Put it on a tray on your lap, and start by roughly cutting the tangled mass into 2–5 cm lengths. It is rather shocking to just cut up this gorgeous glossy silk, but it is too tangled to spin and a tray stops it from going everywhere. Tighten the tension slightly on the break band on your wheel. Join the chopped up throwsters silk onto the primary thread, just like joining on Bombyx mori, letting the loose and crimpy fibres spin together. It won't work unless the fibres are cut into manageable lengths. The shorter the lengths, the more bouclé the effect, and the more firmly it needs to be spun. Throwsters silk is slippery so it needs to be plied with a rough, sticky silk like a mawata or a hand or commercially spun noil. It adds a super texture to both knitting and weaving, dyes like a dream and is great fun to do.

Laps and batts. These sheets of silk are made from poor quality silk fibres, laid out into a thick airy layer. They can be split through the middle, handspun, or used for felt and paper making to give an interesting effect. They can be cut up and make excellent filling.

Gummy Silk. This silk is so named because the sericin has not been washed out. The threads are often waste filament silk. They are strong and springy, and the long lengths can even be threaded through a needle, to embroider or sew with. The gum makes the silk excellent for incorporating into felt and paper making.

Woman with a spindle, fighting knight.

Carrier Rod Waste. This is not a spinning silk, but is made from the loose threads that have got wrapped around the carrier rod which draws the thread from the basins of hot water and onto the reel. Every so often it is slit up the middle to cut it off the rod, and dried. It looks a bit like an old dried runner bean, but when you soak it, it works like a crepe bandage and can be pulled apart, worked and twisted, dyed and cut. There is no limit to the uses of the different silks.

Appendix

Carding Combing and Spinning, the women of the household working in the castle, Boccaccio, *Des cleres et nobles femmes*, Spencer Collection MS 33, f.56r, French c 1470, NY Public Library, NY.

Sericulture

Most people know that silk comes from the silkworm, that the silkmoth lays eggs, hatches into a silkworm, eats mulberry leaves, spins a cocoon, changes into a pupa and then a moth, but there is so much more to the story of the silkworm than that.

Every country, often each district will have different species of silkworms and slightly different methods of handling them. In warm climates like Southern India, the silkworms are multi-voltine and there could be up to seven hatchings a year. In cooler climates where the summer is shorter, then the silkworms could be mono or bi-voltine, and there will be only one or two hatchings each year. Usually, the fewer the hatchings, the larger the cocoons. Silkworms are specially bred to flourish, be disease free and produce the best quality cocoons and silk.

In the spring or when the temperature is around 27 degrees and the new leaves start appearing on the mulberry trees, the silk moth lays around 500 eggs. These may have been laid at the end of the previous season, but they will not hatch until it is the right temperature. If the eggs have been fertilized by the male, they will turn black over the next ten days and hatch into a miniature caterpillar, less than the size of a pinhead.

To give an idea of scale, 30,000 eggs can be contained in a small box, around 8cm in diameter. This is the number of eggs that a farmer can usually manage in a season. Many silk growing districts have research and development facilities and special hatcheries where the eggs are hatched under scrupulously hygienic conditions and they are distributed to the farmers at the second or third instar.

The silkworm goes through four instars, or periods of eating, sleeping and moulting.

When the eggs have just hatched they are placed in a small shallow box, covered with fine gauze and offered the youngest, freshest mulberry leaves. These leaves have been finely cut up and the silkworm will feed continuously for around 36 hours.

It will then stop eating and sleep for twenty-four hours. When it wakes, it will emit a tiny drop of goo from its tail end, to attach itself to a handy leaf. Over the next few hours its skin, like the skin of a snake will split and the silkworm will crawl out, leaving its discarded skin attached to the leaf.

At this stage another layer of gauze is lightly laid over the silkworms. It is covered with fresh mulberry leaves and the silkworms crawl through the mesh and onto the leaves and start eating again. This allows the person caring for the silkworms to remove all the detriment, half chewed leaves and other discarded matter and hygienic conditions are maintained. At each instar the silkworm will eat for a longer period, so that by the time of the fourth instar it will now be about 10cm long, be an ashy-greeny-grey colour and will eat solidly for about ten days. Their container could now be a plastic lined bin, around 4–5 metres long and a metre wide.

Hygiene and strictly controlled conditions are essential because the silkworm is a very fragile creature. Everything must be kept scrupulously clean, the temperature and humidity kept constant, they must have good ventilation and screens up to keep out predators, birds, uzi fly etc. There can be no loud noises, strong smells, or rough handling. A very light gentle touch is required, and the silkworms will flourish.

At the end of the ten days of the fourth instar, the silkworm will start looking around for a suitable place to spin its cocoon. Wigwams of straw, frames of twigs, boxes divided into small sections could be offered, and the silkworm will then experiment with spinning its cocoon.

During the last few weeks of eating, the silkworm has utilized its strong jaws to eat through a mountain of ever larger mulberry leaves. In the first two to three instars, the protein from the leaves is used to enable the silkworm to grow, but during the third and fourth instars that protein will be changed into a liquid silk protein called fibroin and stored in silk ducts running on either side of the silkworm's alimentary tract. These two fine ducts come together under the mouthparts of the silkworm at the spinneret. There the liquid silk is coated with the silk gum called sericin. These two fine threads of liquid silk called brin, harden on exposure to air and the two together form the single thread, the bave. The silkworm moves its head in a figure of eight, touching against the twigs or frame, and as it draws its head back, the liquid silk is drawn out of the ducts.

When it first starts to spin, the thread is uneven and not continuous, but the silkworm soon settles down to spin a fine, even, continuous thread, starting at the outside and gradually enclosing itself inside the cocoon. Although the cocoon is thick and feels firm, it is actually porous, allowing the silkworm to continue to breath. It is astonishing that such a large silkworm can fit inside a small cocoon, but as it spins it empties the silk ducts and contracts.

This is called a green cocoon and usually the cocoons are taken to the cocoon auction market promptly to enable them to be sold on to the reeler. In Southern India there is a cocoon auction almost every single day of the year. Where the species are mono- or bi-voltine, then the markets operate only during the season. In other districts, like in Thailand, all cocoons are delivered to the silk centres where they are weighed and sorted and the farmers paid for their cocoons, the amount dependent on the quality, quantity and condition of the cocoons.

The cocoons are candled, and put over a lit table and the girls work extremely fast sorting them into three main groups. The cocoons that are perfect in every respect are set aside for breeding. The poor, weak, damaged, diseased stained, irregular cocoons, the double ones where the silkworms have got tangled together while they were spinning, and those where the silkworm has died within, are all separated out. These will be used to make various styles of spun silk. The bulk of the cocoons are either snuffed shortly after and stored for later use, or they go to the silk thread reeler.

The cocoons that will be used for breeding are handled very carefully. They are allowed to develop into the pupa stage. This is where the silk moth sheds its skin for the last time within the cocoon. Under the skin is the brown protective layer that allows the silkworm to go through metamorphosis and change into a moth. The silkworm has had large jaws and a strong alimentary system to digest all the protein from the mulberry leaf. It has silk ducts and a spinneret to produce the liquid silk and none of these things are of value to the silk moth. They will atrophy and be replaced by wings, large compound eyes, and gonads that develop either sperm or eggs.

The top of the cocoon is cut off. This allows the silk moth to emerge easily without producing the brown enzyme that would stain the cocoon and without using up too much energy needed for mating. The plump female moth is full of eggs. She just sits there and emits a pheromone to attract the slightly smaller and more agile male to her. They attach themselves tail to tail and over the next few hours he fertilizes her eggs within her body, and gradually she lays her eggs. After three or four days they both die. They are not designed to live any longer. They do not have mouthparts or an alimentary canal system and can neither eat nor drink. They are designed purely to mate and produce eggs, in fact to have a nice day. You cannot make them live one day longer, by tucking them up with cottonwool or feeding them delicious bits of fresh mulberry, they are designed to play their part in the life cycle of the silkworm.

Silk Routes

Traders and travellers left the large vibrant Chinese city of Ch'ang-an (Xi'an) by the West Gate, and travelled over 250 miles, following the Great Wall up the windswept Wei Valley, with its mulberry trees ringing the paddy fields, up what came to be known as the Imperial Highway. The route followed the Huang, the Yellow River, which springs from the K'unlun Mountains, and the Nan Shan or Southern Mountains along the Ganzu Corridor. It skirted the dry expanse of the Gobi Desert by way of Wuwei, Zhangyi, Jiayuquan, and Anxi to Dunhuang, near the Caves of the Thousand Buddhas. It took the Polos forty days to cross the Gobi Desert in the thirteenth century, compared with two and a half days now, by train.

Leaving Dunhuang, there was a choice of two or three trading routes. The T'ien Shan Nan Lu, or the 'Road South of the Celestial Mountains', which begins at the Yumen Kuan or Jade Gate. It goes westwards towards Loulan, skirting the northern edge of the Tarim Basin via the salt-encrusted Lop Desert. Loulan was once an important city, but by the third century the rivers had dried up, making travelling almost impossible. The road proceeded through Karashahr (Yanqi), Wulei, Kucha, (Kuga) Aksu and Kashgar (Kashi), then crossed the treacherous Pamir Mountains to reach Ferghana, known for its splendid horses, fed on the rich alfalfa. This part of the road, called the Royal or Golden Road to Samarkand, continued towards the Iranian Plateau, passing the cities of Samarkand and Bukhara. Both cities had bazaars and caravanserai and were heavily fortified. The route continued to Persia, re-joining the road to Antioch and the Mediterranean at Merv (Mary).

The most northern route left the road at Anhsi, ninety miles east of Dunhuang and crossed parts of the Gobi Desert, to Hami, famous for its melons, dried raisins and sweet wine. The city of Turpan lies 300 feet below sea level, resulting in extreme temperatures; forty degrees Centigrade below in winter and forty degrees above in summer. The route continued alongside the snowcapped peaks of the T'ien Shan or Celestial Mountains to Beshbalik and Almalik, across the semi-arid Dzungarian Basin to Altai and the Golden

Mountains, past the warm salt lake, Issyk Kul, to Tashkent and Samarkand. This route was called the T'ien Shan Pei Lu, the 'Road North of the Celestial Mountains'. It was the easiest route during the Tang and Mongol Dynasties, but as there was seldom peace, it offered easy pickings for bandits.

The southern route was difficult because there were fewer oases where travellers could rest and replenish their provisions, but they were also less likely to be attacked by marauders. The traveller left by the Yang Kuan Gate, going south-west following the 'Road North of the Southern Mountain'. The route skirts the vast Taklimakan Desert, 600 miles across by 250 miles north to south, through Cherchen avoiding the bleak and hostile salt desert around Lop Nor. It crossed the kingdoms of Niya, Wumi, Pishan and Khotan (Hotan), a city renowned for its carpets, taffetas, felts, silks and the finest white and green jade. The route gradually rose towards Yarkand and on to Kashgar (Kashi), 5000 feet above sea level, with its famous Sunday Market, bazaars and orchards. It entered the Karakorum Range, the Tsung-ling or Onion Mountains and the High Pamirs. People believed that it was the wild onions that made them feel ill, but it was really the high altitude and thin air. Hou Han Shu, in 96 CE, wrote feelingly of places like Little Headache, Great Headache and Land of Fever. The route emerged onto the high plateaus, where there was good water and grazing. It was easier now, following the wide river valleys between the Oxus ie the Amu Darya and the Jaxartes or Syr Darya into Western Turkestan, Uzbekistan, Kazakhstan and parts of Afghanistan. Balkh was the half-way point, the crossroad city of the routes to India and the Mediterranean.

The route continued to Balkh, Merv (Mary), Ecbatana, Ctesiphon and Palmyra to the Mediterranean Sea. Some travellers went from Merv to Rayy and Alamut, which was near the modern city of Qazuin. It was the base of the Shi'a sect called the Assassins, led by the Old Man of the Mountains. This route went on to Ecbatana and Hamadan, to the Zagros Mountains and the Mesopotamian cities of Babylon, Seleucia, Ctesiphon and Baghdad.

The route to India went via the Hindu Kush, following the Indus River in Pakistan on the border of Afghanistan and Kashmir, to the Persian Gulf where the goods were loaded into ships sailing to western countries. The Iranian Plateau was often avoided because of the exorbitant taxes and bribes, so merchants went further north to Baku and the Black Sea.

Travellers on the Great Desert Route used two humped Bactrian camels that could carry up to 500 pounds each. The camels walked at a steady three miles per hour, the camel master in absolute control. There are tales of blind camel masters, whose profound knowledge of the route enabled them to sense the right direction and find water from the smell and direction of the wind. Asses, donkeys, yaks and horses were also used, depending on the terrain and climate. Often the caravan travelled at night guided by the stars, to avoid bandits and the blistering heat. Large caravans of several hundred people could take as long as eight or nine years to travel from Ch'ang-an to Persia or northern India and back.

Another branch of the route went to Aleppo and Antioch and into Syria, travelling down the river to the Persian Gulf, to Palmyra the city of Palms, or via Babylon to Petra, Gaza, Alexandria, and the Phoenician cities of Tyre, Sidon and Byblos. Sometimes the choice was to by-pass the cities, and head for the Aegean Sea and Miletus, Ephesus, Smyrna and Troy to Trebizond and Byzantium.

The Northern Route via the Eurasian Steppes went north of the Aural, Caspian and Black Seas, to the Plains of Poland and Germany or south to the Danube Valley into the heart of Europe. It was the easier route with vast plains, fewer mountains, no deserts or harsh climate. It was ideal for wheeled carts, but also for fast marauding nomads.

Marco Polo and Silk

The edition used here is the Everyman's edition, Dent, London 1975, with a foreword by John Masefield. The numbers refer to the three Books and the various chapters.

1:3   Turkey, carpets and silks of crimson and other rich colours are woven here.

1:5   Parts of Georgia and Armenia have been famous for their silk and produce great quantity as well as silk interwoven with gold.

1:5   Tiflis, silken fabrics called ghellie and cloth of gold, Georgians are Orthodox Christians, depend on trade for livelihood, abundance of silk which is woven with gold thread, to make it the most beautiful imaginable.

1:6   Mosul was a vast kingdom with many races of men, Arabs who worship Mohammed, Nestorian and Jacobite Christians. Material known as mosulin woven from silk and gold thread.

1:7   City of Baghdad, (Baldach) where a great variety of materials were worked, silk velluti wrought with gold, cloth of gold, silk damask, brocade and cramoisy, embroidered with many different designs of animals.

1:13 Tauris in Iraq where silk and gold cloth traded. Yazd, another beautiful trading city of Persia, silk woven there is called Yazd, and is much in demand by merchants who make a lot of money by taking it all over the world.

1:14 Kerman, where the women and girls show great imagination in embroidering silks of every colour with birds and animals and other designs. For the noblemen they make enchantingly beautiful curtains as well as bedcovers, cushions and pillows all embroidered with great delicacy.

1:36 Lop Nor, where silk was part of the cremation rituals, coffins covered with silk, small wooden houses hung with silk and cloth of gold.

1:48 Rich folk dressed in sumptuous clothes of gold and silk and precious furs of ermine, sable squirrel and fox, all their belongings beautifully made and very valuable.

1:57 Shang-tu where the Great Khan had hunting tents that were very cleverly made and weatherproofed. His apartments are lined with furs and the tent ropes are silk, tents so costly that no minor king could afford them.

2:7 Outfitting 25,000 prostitutes and members of the court at the Khan's expense.

2:9 For the Khan's personal guard of 12,000 Barons he gave them each thirteen coloured gowns, one for each of the lunar feast days, replaced every 10 years, a total of 156,000 gorgeous garments.

2:11 Great Khan had thirteen even more magnificent outfits, made of richer material and even finer jewels, embroidered with pearls and precious stones, and a priceless gold belt and fine leather embroidered boots, embroidered with silver thread.

2:12 Elephant housings covered with silks embroidered with birds and beasts.

2:16 Khanbalik, where tents are fitted out with taste and skill the tent ropes and cords are all silk.

2.17 Great City of Khanbalik where at least 1,000 cartloads of silk are sent every day, vast quantities of silk cloth and cloth of gold woven there because there is a scarcity of flax, cotton and hemp.

2.18 Mulberry trees are stripped of their bark, and after being steeped and pounded are made into paper money.

2:24 Poor people looked after the silkworms and wove and made garments for the court and as gifts.

2:26 Silk carpets, wrought with silk and gold in a variety of colours.

2:28 Gouza, gold tissue manufactured and the finest kind of gauze.

2.29 In Kingdom of Tái-yuan-fu grows mulberry trees that feed the silkworms.

2.30 City of Píng-yang-fu which is crowded with merchants, mulberry trees are grown and a lot of silk is produced there and the people live by trading.

2:32 Cuncun silk industry, where silk is ferried down the Yellow River, the Great Kara-Moran. Ginger grown in abundance there and large amounts of silk produced.

2:33 Ka-chan-fu, silk manufacturing centre, silk and silk and gold tissue, artisans shops and manufacturing.

2:34 Ken-zan-fu, also engaged in the silk industry. Raw silk is produced in large quantities and tissues of gold.

2.35 Within province of Kun-kin, commerce and manufactures and abundance of silk.

2:49 Chin-ti-gui and Chang-li manufactured silk exported, sent down the river, Pazan-fu had abundant silk, including woven tissues of gold and scarves.

2.51 Chan-gli, large river used to ferry vast quantities of silk, drugs and other valuable articles.

2:52 Tandin-fu, major centre of collection and trade in beautiful silks, large fine city where a lot of extremely rich merchants trade there and an unbelievable amount of silk.

2.57 Pau-ghin and San-yan-fu silk and woven silk and gold tissue. Manji (Shantung) Province of Ngan-King rich province west of Manji, live by trade and craft, have a great variety of silks and they weave cloth of gold.

2.61 Nan-guin in Province of Manji has raw silk and weaves tissue of silver and gold in great abundance.

2.62 Sa-yan-fu has raw silk produced in great quantities and has the finest silks intermixed with gold.

2:65 Chan-ghian-fu, weave tissues of silk and gold.

2:66 Tin-gui-gui, city famous for its raw silk.

2:67 Sin-gui, and Va-gui, impressed by rich merchants and their beautiful gowns and the vast amount of silk manufactured there for both domestic use and other markets.

2:68 Kinsai (Hangchow) luxurious silk clothes, even carriages and barges lined with silk. Silk wrought with gold on the funeral pyres.

2.69 Silk used to pay a tithe to the king.

2:74 Kue-lin-fu, beautiful women wearing luxurious silks.

2:75 Ungen exported most of the silk produced there.

Glossary

Acupictura. Embroidery imitating painting in needlework, finest detail

Ailanthus. American breed of wild silkworm

Anaphe. Wild silk from Africa, Uganda, Botswana, silkworms feed on fig leaves and construct large nests containing clusters of cocoons

Antheraea mylitta. Wild silkworm that feeds on the leaves of the jujube tree in India and spins large compact silver- grey cocoons

Antheraea assama. Wild or semi domesticated silkworm from Assam

Antheraea pernyni. Wild silkworm, native of Mongolia and Northern China, now found in the US, Spain, the Balearic Islands. It feeds on oak leaves and its silk is exported all over the world

Antheraea Yamamai. Japanese silkworm, produces large bright green cocoons with a strong white filament

Antioch. Silk cloth named for the Syrian city, general name for rich silks from the East, sometimes a brocaded silk figured with animals, gazelles and birds whose beaks, heads, feet and roundels on the wings are highlighted in gold thread, famous textile market, 10–12th centuries

Antung. Chinese wild silk, plain weave fabric

Appliqué. Method of attaching individual motifs onto another background

Apparel. Decorated or embroidered silk square or band attached to the cuffs or hem of an alb, amice or other vestment, usually four and sometimes six

Attacas Atlas. Large Indian silk moth, found throughout Java, India, Shi Lanka, Burma, China

Baldachin, baldaquin. Originally a rich patterned silk from Baghdad, or gold canopy or tester suspended over a bed, altar or doorway

Bale. Variable weight of skeined silk. Chinese and Japanese bales weight between 55–65kg (125–140lbs) Italian bales weigh 90kg, (200 lbs)

Barbette, gorget. Band of white linen drawn under the chin and pinned to the hair on either side above the ears, worn by women in 13–14th c

Batik. 'Wax writing', a textile printing method used in Indonesia, Java. Liquid wax is drawn onto the cloth to create the pattern, protecting the areas not to be dyed. It is melted to remove it after the dyeing process is complete

Batting. Thick layer of fluffy silk used for quilting and insulation in quilts and jackets etc

Baves. The twin filament fibres, together with the sericin gum, reeled off the cocoon

Bell. c500gms of Mawata caps made up of layers of broken cocoons, stretched over a bell shaped frame, used for quilting, etc

Bisu. Husks of the cocoons left in the basin after reeling

Blaze. Short fuzzy fibres on the outside of the cocoons

Bliaud (t). Gown, formerly called a *gonelle*, an over tunic with long sleeves, shorter than the chemise, elbow length sleeves went out of fashion around 1050 and succeeded by the long bell sleeves, gored skirt, splits at the sides, worn by both men and women with a belt. Knee length bliaud worn by peasants and soldiers

Bombyx mori. Domesticated silkworm eats mulberry leaves, 95% of world production

Book of silk. Parcel of silk hanks weighing 2 kgs. Japanese silks packed in books of 25–30 skeins. In eighteenth century the guideline was that 3000 cocoons went to make one book

Bouclé. Yarn with looped threads plied onto the core yarn

Bourette. Fr. *Bourre de soie*, meaning floss silk, a dull rough textured yarn or fabric made from *schappe* or degummed silk, spun from the outer-most or inner short fibres of the cocoon, including some of the discarded and crushed chrysalides which present as little brown specks, fairly resistant to wrinkling, shrinks on first washing, dyes well, not colour fast, specially to sunlight, similar to noil

Bourrelet. Padded brim of man's hood, from *bourrer*, to stuff, or padded rolls supporting woman's headdress

Braiding. Narrow flat woven edging or cord

Braies, braccae breeches. Loose drawers worn by men and women, from the 8th c, to early Middle Ages, belted or tied with cord at the waist, the lower edge was tucked into chausses below the knee

Brillante. Weavers' term for the glossiness of the silk

Brin. One of the two filaments of silk extruded by the silkworm via the spinneret located under its jaws. Two brins together, with the gum sericin, harden on exposure to air to form a single silk fibre, known as a bave

Brocade. Elaborately patterned compound weave used for dress or furnishing fabric, similar to damask but multicoloured. Initially required hand manipulation or the use of a drawboy who sat above the loom pulling the warp threads to a set pattern, now done on a mechanical or computerized jacquard loom

Brodaria. Embroiderer

Bullion. Thick twisted fringe, sometimes made from gold, silver or metallic threads

Bum-roll. Padded sausage shaped cushion tied around the waist to hold the skirt out at a fashionable angle

Burse. Stiff square pocket to contain linen cloth used at Holy Communion, also richly embroidered bag for containing a formal seal

Busc, busk, buske. Long pieces of wood, whalebone, ivory, horn, steel etc, placed in the centre front of the corset to keep the body erect

Buskins. Thick soled boot worn by Greeks and Romans, later by Bishops

Calendering. Machine with heated rollers to impress cloth with a moiré or watered effect

Carding. Process to straighten out or tidy loose or matted fibres preparatory to spinning. The fibres are drawn between rollers or wooden panels with a carding cloth of hooked wires

Cartoon. Detailed design for embroidery or tapestry.

Caul. Decorated gold or silver net, fifteenth century headdress enclosing the side hair or plaits, of reticulated gold mesh and decorated with pearls

Cendal, cendaulx, sandal. Lightweight plain weave silk similar to taffeta, often measured by weight rather than width or length, from Asia Minor, popular in the Middle Ages. Initially an expensive fabric, but became cheaper and widely used for linings by the 17th century

Chainse. Early long flared linen tunic, worn under the bliaud, in early Middle Ages, with sleeves and belt

Chapeau bra. Hat, slung over the shoulder by a ribbon, decorative, not designed to be worn

Chaperon. Fr. Combined hood and shoulder cape with liripipe, worn by working men and women out of doors throughout the Middle Ages

Charmeuse. Fine silk satin fabric used for lingerie and heavier weight for evening dresses

Chasuble. Originally a large round cloak with a hole in the centre for the head, recut to be more fiddle-shaped to allow the priest to raise his arms during the Mass. From Latin *casula*

Chausses. Long hose, made of shaped, seamed pieces of fabric, covering the foot and leg, pulled up over the lower part of the braies, gradually became longer, developing into stockings and then tights

Chemise. Fr. General term for fine linen or silk undergarment worn by both men and women, later developed into the loose shirt

Chemisette. Fine silk cloth used to wrap a precious book or icon. In 1807 a chemisette was a style of women's blouse and by 1844 a modesty vest or false front to fill in a low neck

Chenille. Fr. Meaning caterpillar, a velvet or tufted yarn, could be silk, wool or cotton, couched onto the surface of material or woven into rich silk brocades, also used for fringes

Chevron. Pattern of diagonal lines in alternating directions, used as background in medieval embroidery, worked in gold thread with underside couching

Chiffon. Fr, meaning a rag, piece of lace or ribbon. Very fine matt gauzy semi-transparent fabric, made of high twist silk yarns, Crepe georgette, voile, and grenadine are different weight silks in a similar weave

China silk. Lightweight plain weave silk used for linings

Chinoiserie. European designs imitated or inspired by Chinese patterns, important after mid 17th century, applied to all forms or decorative arts, lacquer, furniture, textiles, needlework

Chirimen. Heavy crepe silk, in both plain and woven patterns used for expensive Japanese kimonos

Chrysalis or pupa. Third stage in the metamorphosis of the silkworm, from egg, to caterpillar, to chrysalis to moth, the hard brown inner case inside the cocoon, where the caterpillar changes into a silk moth

Cloak, cloka mantel. Large sleeveless cloak, an outer protective layer of clothing

Cloud-band. Band of pattern imitating a ribbon, widely adopted in Mongol China

Cloth of gold. Elaborate woven silk fabric heavily enriched with gold

Cocoon. Protective shell of silk fibres spun by the silkworm after the fourth instar to protect the pupa during its metamorphosis, when it changes from a caterpillar to a silk moth. It can vary in length from 2 to 4cm, oval or peanut shaped, white, pale green, yellow, cream, or pinkish, depending on food it has eaten and the colour will usually wash out. Wild tussah moths usually form larger, stronger cocoon with a hard outer shell, from palest honey to rich treacly browns due to tannin in the foodstuffs

Coif, coiffe, cale. Fr. closely fitting cap or fitted linen bonnet, tied under the chin, worn under a helmet by men during the early Middle Ages, often worn by judges, lawyers academics

Combing. Process after carding to further refine fibres in preparation for spinning

Compound weave. Complex weave incorporating two or more sets of warp or weft threads, so one set appears on the face and the other on the reverse, eg damask, brocade

Cope, pluvial. Vestment or large semicircular garment, secular or ecclesiastical, fastened across the chest with a brooch or strip of material called a morse. The orphrey or front band was embroidered with cruciform motif with a vestigial hood at the upper back

Coptic textiles. Egyptian textiles produced between the introduction of Christianity and the Arab conquest in 640AD, mostly wool and linen, occasionally silk

Cote-hardie, Cotte hardie, gonella, or paltok. Garment fashionable between 1300–1430 for both men and women, long bodice fitted tight to the hip, buttoned down the front, edge often dagged, full length sleeves could also be a lined fitted dress with short or no sleeves, worn under more formal laced outer garments

Couching. Method of attaching threads, often silk, gold and silver by laying them on the surface of the fabric, and over-sewing using a fine thread

Count. The thickness of a yarn expressed as the length to a fixed weight

Couvre-chefs. Fine linen working women's head covering, including kerchief or veils

Cracows, pike, poulaine. Men's long pointed toed shoes c1360 occasionally so long they were tied to the knee, dated to the arrival of Richard II's Bohemian Queen Anne

Crespinettes, crespine. Box shaped net to enclose the plaited or braided hair above the ears, used by wealthy women cf to a couvre-chef worn by working women

Crape. Stiff dull silk, usually dyed black, fashionable for mourning clothes

Crepe. Tightly twisted yarn in a variety of weights where the individual threads have been twisted in an S or Z manner, then plied in the same or contrary fashion, woven in the gum, has a soft drape and dull matt finish. Variations include crepe de chine, marocain, crepe georgette

Cyclas. Medieval tunic

Dagging, Decopeures. Series of slashes or shaped cuts on the edges of fine, felted woolen garments, created by using specially shaped metal cutters, German origin early 1340, until 1420

Dalmatic. Ecclesiastical vestment with wide square sleeves, slit up the sides, shorter than the alb, worn by deacons assisting the priest at the Mass, and the bishop under his chasuble and the sovereign at his coronation

Damask. Single colour, flat, reversible, compound weave fabric of silk, cotton or linen mixture. By combining free floating warp and weft faced satin or twill weaves with plain weave, the complex pattern of flowers, animal and abstract design is reversed. It predates brocade, possibly named after the Syrian city of Damascus. *Drap de damas de Lucchese* was frequently mentioned in inventories from 1350 onwards

Décolleté. Very low cut neckline

Degumming. Approximately 20% by weight of raw silk is made up of sericin, the gummy substance that coats and protects the silk fibres, making them hard and dull. It is removed by immersion in a hot soap or alkali solution. Sometimes a portion is added back in later finishing stages as weighting, or to condition the fabric

Denier. Comparative thickness of a filament yarn, thread or fibre expressed as the weight in grams to a fixed length of 9,000 metres. The smaller the number the finer the weight of silk

Dtex. Weight in grams of 10,000 metres of silk thread.

Diaper. Compound weave similar to Lampas, where the glossy weft forms the pattern against the plain ground

Diapered. Chequered or diamond hatched background

Diapause. Form of hibernation which allows the chrysalis to lie dormant over winter

Doublet. Men's fourteenth century quilted upper garment

Doubling, plying, folding. Twisting together of two or more yarns, usually in the opposite direction to form a stable fibre

Douppion, Duppion, Duppioni. From duo, meaning two cocoons, a slubbed silk fabric made from two cocoons that have spun together, making it impossible to reel a continuous thread off the cocoon. Handspun and woven in the villages, often dyed into brilliant colours before being woven into plain silks, plaids and stripes. Warp and weft of different colours gives shot silk

Drawing, drafting. Process whereby fibres are gently drawn out from the mass or roving so that an even amount can be spun together to form a thread

Drawloom. Used for weaving the finest figured silks, required a small boy to sit on a platform above the loom, pulling the heddles through which the silks were threaded as required to form the pattern

Duchesse satin. Heavy bridal or ceremonial weight satin

Ecru. Natural coloured tussah silk thrown or woven before being degummed

Ell. An old measure for fabric, in England c45 inches or 1.14m, varies in other countries

Eri. Ailanthus wild silk moth native of Bengal, Assam and Arrindi, species include **Philosamia** ricini and Philosamia cynthia, Samia cynthia, all polyvoltine producing up to seven generations each year, feeding on castor oil plants, producing loose flossy cocoons, orange-red or white, neither can be reeled but must be spun and nowadays both are partly cultivated indoors

Faille. Thick soft taffeta style silk, horizontal weft ribbed with or without a moiré finish

Fanon. Maniple or narrow strip of material worn on the left forearm by the priest, deacon and sub-deacon

Fardel, torsello. Long canvas covered bale of skeined, raw or woven silk, a quarter of the weight that an animal can carry in each pannier bag. The emblem of the Lucchese silk merchants.

Farthingale. Fr. *vertugade*, canvas or linen petticoat stiffened with whalebone hoops tied round the waist to hold out the skirt, began in Spain in late fifteenth century

Ferronerie. Decorative curved design like wrought iron work, often voided on velvet

Fibula. Clasp to fasten cloak, used since pre-historic times, often made of gold and richly decorated.

Fibres. Any long fine matter, natural or man-made that when laid together and twisted, can form a flexible yarn or thread

Fibroin. Amino acid based liquid silk that the silkworm ejects from its spinneret when spinning its cocoon, hardens on exposure to air to form silk fibre

Fibula (e). Brooch, to fasten draped garments

Figured silks. Where the design is woven into the fabric, rather than embroidered on it

Filament. Continuous thread or fibre, natural or man-made. In silk it is the continuous thread as reeled off the cocoon

Filature. Factory or community based centre where silk cocoons are boiled and the silk reeled

Filé, fillet. Smooth thread composed of a core of silk or linen thread twisted with another metallic gilded membrane, or gold band to be worn on the head

Fitchets. Slit or opening in the surcoat over the hip bone, so that the wearer had access to money or keys while keeping them hidden

Float. Weft or warp yarn, carried over the surface of two or more threads

Floss, Frissons. Waste short lengths of silk fibre taken from the outside and innermost parts of the cocoon, often only lightly twisted and used in embroidery, sometimes laid on or couched

Flyer. An attachment to a spinning wheel or machine that allows the spun fibres to be wound and spaced on the reel automatically

Foulard. Light weight twill woven silk, used for ties and scarves

Frontlet. Fr. Front section of a women's headdress, introduced c1485, usually loop of black velvet, worn across the forehead

Fuji. Firmly woven plain silk, originating in Japan

Gabardine. Originally a woollen cloak, now a term for a firm twill woven fabric, often silk or wool

Garde-corps. 14th century tunic, or garment worn over a surcoat, widely flared, lined, sleeved or sleeveless, worn calf length by men and ankle length by women, or corset which by 1250 was called a cote-hardi, sleeveless or wide elbow length sleeves

Gauze, gaze. Very fine sheer stiffened silk, often used for millinery, said to have come originally from Gaza

Georgette. Heavier weight chiffon style fabric, with a soft drape and handle, woven from tightly twisted two or three ply crepe yarns

Gilded membrane, parchment. Flat gilded strips, woven or embroidered into garments

Gipon. Early undergarment, prototype of doublet, initially referred to as undertunic

Godet, gore, gusset. Triangular piece of material set into the skirt to provide flare or the underarm for ease of movement

Gold thread. Earliest are membranes, fine strips of gilded fish skin or animal gut, later wire or flat strips, wafer thin beaten gold wrapped around a silk core. After the Middle Ages pure gold was replaced with silver gilt with a coating of gold, speciality of Cologne

Gold work. Couched embroidery, earliest examples probably of Chinese origin

Gonnella, gonna, sottana, gamurra, camora. Simple unlined dress worn by all women, whatever class, mostly wool sometimes with silk sleeves, worn over a light chemise, developed from French into English word gown

Gorget. White throat covering worn with the wimple

Gown. L. toga, or Fr. houppelande, outerwear sleeved garment worn by both sexes from c1360, shape and length changed, some had upper arm band with a tippet hanging down

Grain. Smallest unit of weight being 1/5,760th pound (Troy) or 1/7,000th pound (avoirdupois) Dates from 1542 and was the weight of the centre of an ear of corn, used formerly as a measurement for cotton and linen

Graine. Fr. Silkworm seed, or eggs

Great Wardrobe. Section of a royal medieval household that dealt with clothing and textiles, furnishings, dry goods, spices, candles etc

Green cocoons. Fresh cocoons

Grege, Soie grege. Plain weave, dull silk fabric, with some gum still in it

Grenadine. Very fine silk and or woollen dress fabric, made from highly twisted organzine silk, possibly originally from Grenada in Spain

Gros de Naples, Tours. Very heavy corded silk made in Italy

Grosgrain. Plain ribbed silk

Ground. Background of the design or pattern

Gum, Sericin. Gummy substance which causes the two brin or filaments to cling together. Needs to be removed by being softened in hot water

Gynaeceum. Women's weaving quarters during Roman and Byzantium period, but later not exclusively feminine

Habutai, Habutae, Habotai. Japanese name for their plain woven lightweight silk fabrics, popular for scarves and linings

Haincelin. Short houppelande, fashionable in fifteenth century France

Hank. Skein of silk taken from the reel, tied in a number of places and twisted into a figure of eight

Hard spin, ply. Fibres with many of twists to the inch

Heddle. Set or parallel strings or wires, with a central eye, threaded in a particular pattern sequence, for separating and guiding the warp threads on the loom

Hennin. High steeple headdress, fashionable in fourteenth and fifteen centuries popular in Burgundy, originally a derogatory term

Henque, heuque. Sleeveless men's over garment with slits up the sides to let the arms through, connected with liveries and sewn with badges, a kind of cloak

Honan, Hunan. Chinese province of Honan, handwoven silk fabric, often incorporating both domesticated silk for the warp and wild silk for the weft. Natural soft creamy colour that absorbs the dyes of the wild and domestic silk differently

Hose. Well shaped leg garment often striped or parti-coloured, fur lined in winter, foot portion soled, making indoor shoes unnecessary, by 1370–80 the legs had joined to become tights and extended nearly to waist level, attached to the shorter under tunic by laces and eyelet holes all around the body, requiring a braguette or codpiece, attached by points and ties

Houppelande. A characteristic garment 1380–1450, later known as the gown, fitted the shoulders and was loose below, belted forming pleats, length varied, extremely wide sleeves, high upright collar, edge dagged, made of rich material or wool, often lined with fur

Jacquard. Loom, developed in France in 1801–3 by Joseph-Marie Jacquard, born in Lyon in 1752 died 1834, uses a sequence of punched and blank space cards laced together which allows the thread to be raised to weave complicated and delicate patterns such as damask and brocades making drawboy superfluous

Jerkin. Originally a sleeveless outer doublet

Journeyman. Man or woman who had completed their years of apprenticeship and now qualified and free to work for wages

Kekolymena. Highest grade of Byzantine silk, manufactured in the Imperial Workshop for the use of the Emperor or as state gifts. Was a Byzantine term that meant 'forbidden cloth' because only available to selected people and heavy penalties for disobedience

Kirtle. Women's chemise or petticoat, an inner garment, worn over the shirt or smock, early form of corset, replaces tunic between 1300–1400

Laid work. Embroidery, long threads often of floss silk or cord laid on the surface and fixed at points with couching stitches, to outline the pattern

Lamé. Rich fabric where most of the pattern is made up with gold or silver threads

Lampas or diasprum. Compound figured weave, usually in silk, in which supplementary wefts and warps are added to the face of the fabric. The pattern is formed by the weft floats woven into the main ground and carried at the back. Now woven on a jacquard loom and used in furnishings

Lappets. Thin strips of material hanging down the back of a Bishop's mitre, or to a band around the upper arm, or attached to the sides of a ladies cap in the 18th and 19th century

Liripipe, cornetes, becchetto. Long hanging tail from the hood of the chaperon, sometimes so long it had to be knotted or wound round the hat, often padded, 13–14th century

Lucca. Italian city in Tuscany, major centre of medieval silk production in 13th century became the first town in Northern Italy to admit Muslim silk weavers

Lustre. Reflection of light from the surface of the fibre or yarn, directly proportional to the straightness of the fibres and to the tightness or looseness of the spinning and plying. Lustre is reduced by unevenness of the fibre surface, or poor finishing

Maniple, Hanon. Thin strip of cloth worn over the left forearm by the priest, deacon or subdeacon at the Mass. Originally designed for wiping the head or brow, but became increasingly decorated, now purely ornamental with ends often of cloth of gold

Mantua. Fr. word Manteau a silk gown or petticoat or Mantua in Italy

Matelassé. Fr. quilted, padded or stuffed silk fabric

Mawata. Pierced cocoons, opened up after soaking in hot water to soften the sericin, then stretched over a dome or square frame, to dry. The caps or handkerchiefs can be dyed, useful for spinning, stuffing or in quilting

Mercer. Dealer in silks and other textiles

Micron. One-thousandth of a millimetre, written as ∞ (pronounced mew). 1 micron = 1/25,400th inch

Mille Fleurs. Tapestry and illuminated manuscript design where the ground is scattered with thousands of realistic flowers with courtly subjects, typical of the International Gothic style, 15–16th century

Miniver. Fur of the squirrel, arranged in shield-like rows, reserved for the nobility

Mitre. Doubled pointed hat, lappets hanging down the back, worn by a Bishop

Mixed silk. Woven fabric with less than 100 percent pure silk, combined with linen, cotton, wool, ramie in the weave or spun with the silk

Moiré. Silk taffeta or ribbed silk that has been drawn through heated and ridged rollers, which imprints a wavy watered appearance to the pattern, light weight or heavier for furnishing. Other silk moiré fabrics include faille or *poult de soie*, or *moiré d'Angleterre*

Momme. Japanese unit of weight equivalent to 3.756gms indicating the weight and fineness of the yarn per square metre, abbreviated to mm

Monovoltine. Silkworm species that produces one generation per year

Mordant. Addition of a chemical to the yarn or dye-bath to assist the dye to penetrate the silk and help it remain colour fast

Moriculture. Cultivation of mulberry orchards

Mousseline. Very lightweight silk

Muga. Soft, fine, brilliant, wild silk produced by the silk moth Antheraea assamensis in Assam, Northern India

Multivoltine. Silkworm species that produce a number of generations each year

Nib. Lump of raw silk, formed by the collection of waste from boiling the cocoons

Noil. See Bourette

Opus Anglicanum. English Work, fine Medieval all-over embroidery, done in England between 900 and 1500 CE, high period between 1250–1350, featuring underside couching technique, gold work, pictorial, arcading, utilized in ecclesiastic, court, livery, furnishings

Organza. Sheer, stiff, dull finished silk fabric, dyed in the yarn before the gum is removed

Organzine. High twist fine filament silk thread, used for warp

Or nué. Shaded gold laid work embroidery, where the gold thread is caught using finest silk thread, at varying distance and intensities to provide shadow effect

Orphrey. Decorative embroidered cross placed centrally on a chasuble or cope, gold embroidered work, cloth of gold

Paj. Lightweight Chinese plain weave silk, from 5–8 mm or 20–24grams

Pall. Elaborate textile often embroidered and fringed to cover a coffin during the funeral ceremonies

Paltok. Male garment introduced in 1360s, still worn in 1390s, made of wool or silk, and very short, used as an anchor for hose, meant to be seen, often embroidered with gold

Pane(s). Separate strips of fabrics, joined top and bottom for hangings or garments so the underlying fabric can be seen or pulled through to decorative effect, 16th century

Pamphile. Daughter of Plateus, said to have discovered silk on the Greek Island of Cos

Panné velvet. Velvet or velour in which the pile lies flat, creating a lustrous polished surface

Parti-coloured. Garments divided vertically into two colours, eg one leg red and the other blue, fashionable from twelfth to fifteenth centuries

Partlet. Detachable collar or yoke, embroidered or jewelled

Passementerie. Fr. braids and tassels, trimmings and other woven decorative items, 16th century metal thread lace

Pattens. Wooden or cork soled overshoes for wearing outside, held onto the foot by strap or buckles, to lessen the wear on soft leather soles of hose

Peascod belly. Padded bottom portion of doublet to give a paunch shape Sp, second half 16thc

Pebrine. Disastrous silkworm disease that almost wiped out the industry in Europe and the Near East in the mid 19th century, only controlled when Louis Pasteur discovered the hereditary cause

Pecia. Measure of silk cloth cf *pannus*, for woollen cloth

Pelisse, pelisson, pelican. Long fur lined and padded circular cloak worn by women during the Middle Ages

Pile weave. Furry surface to the fabric made by extra warp or weft threads, later cut, as in velvet and corduroy

Plastron. Metal breastplate in armour, then name given to fur neck infills, and later decorative stomachers

Points, laces, Aglet, aiglet, aiguillette. Metal tipped laces or ribbons for attaching hose to breeches, doublet to hose, sleeves to doublet, used as a fastening

Pounce. Method of pricking out a design from a piece of paper or parchment, so that the charcoal or other dust goes through the holes and outlines the pattern on the fabric underneath

Pourpoint, gipon. Fr. for garment, became the doublet, implied military use, became shorter making a hip belt impossible and so a tight waist became fashionable again, padded on the chest and shoulders, very high neckline under the ears, trimmed with fur, variety of sleeves

Prin, quill. Yarn filled bobbins or spools held in the shuttle for weaving

Ply, Plying. Twisting together of two or more spun threads, usually in the opposite direction, to make a stable yarn

Poly voltine. Silkworm types that have many generations each year

Pongee. Chinese word for hand-woven, a soft creamy coloured spun plain weave silk fabric, woven from tussah silk or mixed tussah and Bombyx mori fibres, good washing, often used for blouses and summer garments, sometimes bleached or dyed

Pure silk. One hundred percent silk thread or fabric, without extra salts used for weighting, or other fibres added

Raw silk. Domesticated Bombyx mori or tussah silk with the gum, sericin still in it, which retards the acceptance of dye, so it is usually removed, not the same as wild silk which is only tussah

Reeling. Drawing off or unwinding fibres from a number of silk cocoons onto a large reel or wheel, later wound into skeins

Resist dyeing. Wax or clay is applied to the fabric or the fabric tied into tight bundles to stop the dye penetrating in that area, eg ikat

Robe. Set of three to six matching garments, including tunics, mantles, cloaks

Roving. Very soft and loosely held together rope of silk fibres from which the spinner or machine draws out the fibres to the thinness required to spin the chosen yarn

Samite. Rich weft faced compound twill, a heavy lustrous satin-like silk fabric, mentioned in medieval texts as being used for clothing, ceremonial garments, furnishings, funeral palls, occasionally patterned, often interwoven with threads of gold and silver, originally produced in the East and used for royal robes and ecclesiastical garments

Sand washed silk. Silk which has had additional chemical processes to make it very soft with a good drape and handle, giving it a 'bloom' effect, popular in the 1980's but it water spotted very badly and the chemicals weakened the silk, not popular now

Sarsenet. Fine light silk used for veils, appeared in old inventories, apparently made originally by the Saracens in the thirteenth century, fashionable in the West from the fifteenth century for dresses and trimmings

Satin. Highly lustrous smooth-faced silk fabric of various weights from very light for lingerie to very heavy duchesse satin for wedding gowns and furnishings

Satin stitch. Long, smooth, closely set embroidery stitch designed to cover the surface

Scarlet, escarlate. Top quality woollen cloth, made in a brilliant hue, later name for colour red

Schappe. Rather smelly fermentation process to remove the gum sericin from the silk, done well outside the town or up in the mountains, needs a steady supply of clean running water

Scroop. Rustling sound made by silk taffeta that has been heavily weighted with metallic salts. These salts can weaken the fibre, and their use is these days severely controlled

Seed, graine. Silkworm eggs

Sendal. Widely used strong plain weave stiff taffeta silk used for banners. Finer qualities used for headdresses

Sericin. See Gum

Sericulture. Cultivation of mulberry trees and the care and nurture of silkworms to produce cocoons and reelable silk

Shantung. Wild silk from Northern China, fibre made into a tough wearable slubbed fabric

Shibori. Japanese tie-dye

Shot silk. Silk woven from two contrasting colours, one for the weft and one for the warp, resulting in an iridescent sheen

Slashing. Fashion for making decorative cuts in fabrics, so the contrasting under garment shows through

Slips. Embroidered motifs which are appliquéd onto the main fabric, used especially on heavy silk or velvet hangings, banners or vestments

Slub silk. Small irregular knobs on the thread, in both warp and weft on both wild tussah silk and Bombyx mori types

Singles. First yarn spun for a thread

Sliver, rolag. Untwisted fibres prepared by carding, combing, or some mechanical means in preparation for spinning

Spangle. Small shiny glittering objects sewn onto fabric to give a sparkly effect

Spindle. Thin stick, weighted at one end, twirled by the spinner so the fibres are drawn out and twisted together to form a thread

Spinning. Process using a wheel, spindle or appropriate machine to draw out fibres and give them sufficient twist to hold together to form a single thread

Split stitch. Very fine medieval embroidery stitch where the lightly twisted silk is pierced at each stitch, used for finest detailing of faces, etc

Sprang. Ancient form of pre-knitting, to make a decorative mesh fabric

Spun silk. Short lengths, waste or non-filament silk which is carded, combed and spun to form a silk fibre, later woven

Stamped velvet. Fabric with a pattern stamped into it by feeding it through incised heated rollers

Staple. Fibres short enough to measure in inches or centimetres

Stomacher. Separate stiff decorative V shaped panel attached to the woman's bodice, often extensively decorated with embroidery lace, ribbons and jewels, ending in a point below the waist, Spanish origin

Stencil. Method of imprinting a pattern on fabric, used since 500CE by Chinese and Japanese

Stifle. Method of killing the silkworm pupa by steam or heat before the silk moth breaks through and emerges from the cocoon

Stole. Narrow woven or embroidered scarf worn over the shoulders

Sumptuary laws. Designed to prevent luxurious or flamboyant living by controlling expenditure clothes etc, so person's position and rank are clearly defined

Surcote, super tunic. Originating from a knights tabard, by 1220 was a loose sleeveless garment with large armholes, three quarter length, showing the bliaud below, worn by both sexes in 14th c, women had a sleeveless form, with scooped out armholes showing the outline of their body shoulder to hip, called a *surcote overte*

Surah. Glossy medium weight silk often twill weave, used for ties, also known as foulard, initially from India

S or Z spin, S or Z twist. Direction in which fibres are spun to form a continuous thread

Tabard. Sleeveless or short-sleeved tunic worn over armour to deflect the sun, often highly decorated for ceremonial occasions, displaying coats of arms, heraldic devices

Tabbi. Striped silk, but later for silks with a wavy or watered appearance

Tabby. Simplest plain weave, of alternating weft and warp threads, can be yarn or piece dyed, sometimes streaked or watered, a base for printed designs, said to derive from Attabi a textile producing area near Baghdad, used for taffeta, muslin, and other fibres as well as silk

Taffeta. Impermeable oiled silk, or weighted plain weave making it stiff and rustle

Tartar cloth. Silk from Tartary or old China, in 14th century used to describe figured exotic silks patterned in gold with birds, animals and mythical beasts

Thread count. Number of warps or weft per unit width or length to form a fabric

Throwing. Second major process after reeling, groups of three to ten silk filaments off the cocoons, the fibre is twisted and doubled together, to make a more durable yarn

Tippet. Long hanging pendant streamers attached to upper arm of sleeves, hat

Tiraz. Name both for the Arabic and Spanish Moslem textile workshops and the decorative woven bands made there, sometimes with Arabic Kufic inscription, usually religious or the names of Sultans or noblemen, woven in gold or coloured thread

Tissage. Fr. for weaving

Tram. Thick, barely twisted silk fibres, used in embroidery and weaving in the weft to give a ribbed effect. In embroidery it is the preparatory laid threads on the canvas

Trompe l'oeil. Pictorial deception, making the viewer think it is the real thing, when it is only a two dimensional representation of the item

Trunk-hose. Medieval garment, from the waist to the knee, later known as breeches,

Tussah. Silk from wild or undomesticated silk moths usually fibre more ribbon-like in cross section and darker and coarser than Bombyx mori

Twill. Weave based on three or more ends and picks, offset, to give a diagonal effect used for surahs, herringbone and diamond patterns

Underside couching. Method of securing gold thread to the surface of the fabric whereby the silk securing thread pulls the gold thread through to the back of the fabric, in tiny loops ensuring that less gold thread is wasted and giving the face of the fabric the smoothest and shiniest appearance. Extensively used in Medieval embroidery

Vair. Squirrel fur, one of the most valued furs in the Middle Ages

Velours, Plush. Tightly set napped or brushed silk, V*elours de Gene* is a polychrome floral voided Genoese velvet, not only made in Genoa, *Velours de Venise* and *Velours de Florence*

Velvet. Pile silk, of ancient origin, used for both clothing and furnishings, the extra warp threads form loops when they are laid over wires, later cut. They can be all pile, voided where only parts are of pile are cut to give a sculptural effect as in *alto-e-basso* or pile on pile velvet, the plain areas can be plain, satin or brocaded, with metallic and gold threads used to heighten the design. In 1830 at Lyon a new method was devised where two cloths were woven simultaneously, the loops joining them together, later cut to separate the two fabrics, leaving both with a pile

Venetians. Wide baggy balloon shaped breeches

Vestments. Ecclesiastical clothing worn by officiating members of the Christian church, sets can include mitre, pallium, cope, dalmatic, maniple, stole, alb, chasuble, tunicle, some items traditionally silk, some embroidered, colour coordinated according to the seasonal religious festivals

Voile. Fine silk, cotton or wool semi-transparent fabric woven with double or triple threads

Warp. Lengthwise threads laid on the loom to weave a fabric

Warp-faced. Where additional warp threads are incorporated into the fabric so that the weft threads are completely covered

Weft. Crosswise threads laid in between alternating warp threads to form the fabric, also called woof, picks, or filling threads

Weft-faced. Cloth, usually with a finer and closer set warp, and where the weft of filling yarns are packed down to completely cover the warp threads

Weighting. Chemicals or metallic salts, gums, or sugars added to silk, or returned to silk after scouring, to improve appearance, handle or for special effects

Wild silk. Silk fabric, produced by undomesticated wild silkworms, Saturniidae giant silkworms, tussah, eri, muga, Attacus. The moths are generally much larger than the Bombyx mori, brown in colouring, with an 'eye' on the wings

Wimple. Fine piece of linen or silk worn by older women in the Middle Ages, covering the head, neck, started as simple square tucked into the front of the gown for modesty, developed into the barbette or wimple, pinned to the hair above the ears, then draped around the throat

Woodcut. Print, often with a picture, made from a wooden block where all the areas not intended to carry ink have been cut away

Bibliography

Abrams, Annie, "Women Traders in Medieval London", *Economic Journal 26,* (1916)

Amt, Emilie, *Women's Lives in Medieval Europe: A Source Book*, ed. Routledge, New York, London. 1993

Anderson, Bonnie S & Judith P Zinsser, *A History of their Own, Women in Europe from Prehistory to the Present*, Vol 1. Penguin Books, England, 1988

Anquetil, Jacques, *Soie en Occident*, Flammarion, Paris & New York, 1995

Arano, Luisa Cogliati, *The Medieval Health Handbook, Tacuinum Sanitatis*, George Braziller, New York, 1976

Arnold, Janet, *A Handbook of Costume*, Macmillan, 1973

Arizzoli-Clementel, Pierre, *The Textile Museum, Lyon*, 1990

Aruga, Hisao, *Principles of Sericulture*, Translated from the Japanese, New Age International (P) Publishers, New Delhi, 2001

Askari, Nasreen & Liz Arthur, *Uncut cloth*, Merrell Holberton, London, 1999

Bachrach, Bernard S, *Liber Historiae Francorum* ed and trans. Coronado Press, 1973

Baer, Ann, *Medieval Woman, Village Life in the Middle Ages*, Michael O'Mara Books, 1996

Bagley, J J, *Life in Medieval England*, Batsford, 1971

Baker, Derek, ed. *Medieval Women*, Published for the Ecclesiastical Society by Basil Blackwell, Oxford 1978

Baker, Patricia, *Islamic textiles*, British Museum Press 1995, NSEG

Ball, J N, *Merchants and Merchandise, The Expansion of Trade In Europe, 1500–1630*, Croom Helm, London, 1977

Barraclough, Geoffrey, *The Medieval Papacy*, Library of European Civilization, Thames & Hudson, 1979

Barham, Henry, *An Essay Upon the Silkworm*, 1719, reprinted Robin & Russ Handweavers, 1988

Baricco, Alessandro, *Silk*, Panther, 1997

Barron, Caroline M & Anne F Sutton, ed. *Medieval London Widows*, 1300–1500, Hambledon Press, London & Rio Grande, 1994

Barron, Caroline, *The Medieval Guildhall of London*, Corporation of London, Guildhall, 1974.

Basing, Patricia, *Trades and Crafts in Medieval Manuscripts*, British Library, 1990

Bautier, Robert-Henri, *The Economic Development of Medieval Europe*, Thames & Hudson, London, 1971

Bennett, H S, *The Pastons and Their England*, Canto, Cambridge University Press, 1995

Bennett, Judith M & Elizabeth A Clark, Jean F O'Barr, Anne Vilen & Sarah Westphal-Wihl, ed, *Sisters and Workers in the Middle Ages*, The University of Chicago Press, Chicago & London, 1989

Bergreen, Laurence, *Marco Polo From Venice to Xanadu*, Quercus, London, 2008

Bertin-Guest, Josiane, *Chinese Embroidery, Traditional Techniques*, B T Batsford, 2003

Birbari, Elizabeth, *Dress in Italian Painting, 1460–1500*, John Murray, 1975

Black, J Anderson, Madge Garland and Frances Kennett, *A History of Fashion*, Orbis 1990.

Bonavia, Judy, Sarah Jessup, & Edward Juanteguy, *The Silk Road from Xi'an to Kashgar*, Passport Books, NTC Publishing Group, Lincolnswood, Ill. USA, 1993

Boorstin, Daniel, *The Discoverers*, Penguin, 1983

Boraigh, Dr., G. ed. *Lectures on Sericulture*. SBS Publishers Distributors, Bangalore, India, 1994

Boulnois, L, *The Silk Road*, Translated by Dennis Chamberlain, George Allen & Unwin, London, 1966

Bradfield, N, *Historical Costumes of England 1066–1968*, Eric Dobby Publishing, 1970

Brooke, Iris, *A History of English Costume*, Methuen, London, 1979

Brown, Judith and Jordan Goodman, 'Women and Industry in Florence', in the *Journal of Economic History*, No 40, 1980

Buss, Chiara, ed *Seta, il Novecento a Como*, Fondazione Antonio Ratti, Silvana Editoriale, 2001

Cansdale, C H C, *Cocoon Silk, A Manual for those employed in the Silk Industry and for Textile Students*, Sir Isaac Pitman & Sons, Ltd, London, 1937

Chatterton, Jocelyn, *Chinese Silks and Sewing Tools*, Jocelyn Chatterton, 2002

Chung, Young Y, *The Art of Oriental Embroidery, History, Aesthetics and Techniques*, Bell & Hyman, 1980

Chung, Young Y, *Silken Threads, A History of Embroidery in China, Korea, Japan and Vietnam*, Harry N Abrams, New York, 2005

Clayre, Alasdair, *The Heart of the Dragon*, Dragonbooks, 1985

Coss, Peter, *The Lady in Medieval England*, 1000–1500, Sutton Publishing, 1998

Cossalter, Elisabeth & Jean-Marc Blache, *Au Fil de la Soie*, Didier Richard

Cotterell, Arthur, *China: A Concise Cultural History*, Guild Publishing, London, 1988

Cotterell, Arthur, *The First Emperor of China*, Penguin Books, 1989

Crowfoot, Elisabeth, Frances Pritchard & Kay Staniland. *Textiles and Clothing c1150–1450, Medieval Finds from Excavations in London*: 4, Museum of London, HMSO, 1992

Dale, M K 'The London Silkwoman of the 15th Century' in *The Economic History Review*, No 4, 1932–34

Dalrymple, William, *In Xanadu, A Quest*, Flamingo, London, 1990

Dandin, S B & Jayant Jayaswai, K Giridhar, *Handbook of Silk Technologies*, Central Silk Board, Bangalore, 2001

D'Assailly, Gisele, *Ages of Elegance, Five Thousand years of Fashion and Frivolity*, MacDonald – London, 1968

Dean, Beryl, *Ecclesiastical Embroidery*, Batsford, 1960

Donnell, E W. 'Beguines and Beghards' in *Medieval Culture, with Special Emphasis on the Belgium Scene*, New Brunswick New Jersey, 1954

Douglas, David C and George W Greenaway, *English Historical Documents II 1042–1189* 2nd edition, Eyre Methuen, London, 1981

Drege, Jean-Pierre and Emil M Buhrer, *The Silk Road Saga*, Facts on File, New York, Oxford, 1989

Duby, Georges, ed *A History of Private Life, II Revelations of the Medieval World*, Harvard University Press, 1988

Ennen, Edith, *The Medieval Woman*, translated by Edmund Jephcott, Basil Blackwell, Oxford, 1989

Erler, Mary & Maryanne Kowaleski, *Women & Power in the Middle Ages*, University of Georgia Press, 1988

Evans, Joan, *The Flowering of the Middle Ages*, Guild Publishing, London, 1985

Ewing, Elizabeth, *Dress and Undress, A History of Women's Underwear*, Batsford, London, 1978

Fairbanks, John K and Edwin O Reischauer, *China Tradition and Transformation*, George Allen and Unwin, London, Boston, 1979

Favier, Jean, *Gold & Spices, The Rise of Commerce in the Middle Ages*, Holmes & Meier, New York, London, 1998

Feltwell, Dr John *The Story of Silk*, Alan Sutton, 1990

Fletcher, Joan, *Silk in New Zealand*, NZSW & Woolcrafts Soc, Inc

Foster, Sir William, *England's Quest of Eastern Trade*, Pioneer History Series

Franck, Irene M & David M Brownstone, *The Silk Road, A History*, Facts on File, New York, 1986

Fraser-Lu, Sylvia, *Handwoven South East Textiles from Asia*, Oxford University Press

Gaddum, H T & Co, *Silk*, 1979

Gardiner, Brian O C, *A Silkmoth Reader's Handbook*, The Amateur Entomologist, Vol 12, 1982

Garrett, Valery M, *Traditional Chinese Clothing*, Oxford University Press, 1991

Garrett, Valery M, *Mandarin Squares*, Oxford University Press, 1990

Gelber, Harry, *The Dragon and the Foreign Devils, China and the World, 1100BC to the Present*, Bloomsbury, 2007

Gernet, Jacques, *A History Of Chinese Civilization*, CUP Transl. J R Foster, 1982

Gies, Frances & Joseph, *Women in the Middle Ages, The lives of Real Women in a vibrant age of Transition*, Perennia Library, Harper & Row, New York, 1978

Gies, Joseph and Frances, *Merchants and Moneymen, The Commercial Revolution, 1000–1500*, Arthur Barker Ltd, London, 1972

Glazier, Richard, *Historic Textile Fabrics*, B T Batsford, London, 1923

Ginsburg, Madeleine, *Illustrated History of Textiles*, Studio Edition, 1991

Goldberg, P J P, *Women, Work and Life Cycle in a Medieval Economy, 1300–1520* Clarendon Press, Oxford, 1992

Goldberg, P J P, *Women in Medieval English Society*, Sutton Publishing, 1997

Goodrich, L Carrington, *A Short History of the Chinese People*, Harper Torchbooks, Harper & Row, 1963

Hafter, Daryl M, ed. *European Women and Pre Industrial Craft*, Indiana University Press, Bloomington & Indianapolis, 1995

Hali Publishing, *Silk & Stone, The Art of Asia*, London, 1996

Hanawalt, Barbara A, ed. *Women and Work in Preindustrial Europe*. Indiana

University Press, Bloomington, 1986

Hao, Qian, & Chen Heyi & Ru Suichu, *Out of China's Earth, Archaeological Discoveries in the People's Republic of China*, Frederick Muller Limited, London and China Pictorial, Beijing

Harris, Jennifer, *5000 Years of Textiles* British Museum Press, 1993

Harte, N B & K G Ponting, *Cloth & Clothing in Medieval Europe, Essays in Memory of Professor E M Carus-Wilson*, Pasold Studies in Textile History, 2. Heinemann Educational Books, London, 1983

Harte, N B & K G Ponting, ed. *Textile History And Economic History, Essays in Honour of Julia de Lacy Mann*, Manchester University Press, 1973

Hedin, Sven, *Through Asia*, 2 vols Methuen, 1898

Heden, Sven, *The Silk Road*, George Routledge & Sons, London, 1938

Heer, Friedrich, *Europe 1100–1350*, Weidenfeld, London, 1993

Hegyi, Klara, *The Ottoman Empire in Europe*, Corvina, 1986

Herlihy, David, *Medieval Households*, Harvard University Press, 1985

Herrin, Judith, *A Medieval Miscellany*, Weidenfeld & Nicholson, 1999

Holmes, George, ed, *The Oxford Illustrated History of Medieval Europe*, BCA, 1992

Holmes, George, *Europe: Hierarchy and Revolt 1320–1450*, Fontana History of Europe, 1984

Houston, Mary G, *Ancient Greek, Roman and Byzantine Costume*, Adam and Charles Black, London, 1947

Houston, Mary G, *Medieval Costume in England & France, 13th 14th and 15th centuries. A Technical History of Costume, Vol III*. A & C Black, London, 1979

Howell, Martha C, *Women, Production and Patriarchy in Late Medieval Cities.*, University of Chicago Press, 1986

Hoyt, Robert S & Stanley Chodorow, *Europe in the Middle Ages*, 3rd ed, Harcourt Brace Jovanovich, New York, 1976

Hufton, Olwen, *The Prospect Before Her, A History of Women in Western Europe, Vol 1, 1500–1800*, Fontana Press, 1997

Humble, Richard, *Marco Polo*, Book Cub Associates, London, 1975

Huyghe, Rene, gen ed. *The Larousse Encyclopedia of Byzantine & Medieval Art*, Paul Hamlyn, 1958

Inalrik, Halil with Donald Qualaert, *An Economic and Social History of the Ottoman Empire, 1300–1914*, 1994

Ingram, Elizabeth, ed, *Threads of Gold, Embroideries and Textiles in York Minster*, Pitkin Pictorials, Andover, 1987

Ingram Hill, Rev Canon D, *Canterbury Cathedral*, Bell & Hyman, 1986

Jacoby, David, *Trade and Commodities and Shipping in the Medieval Mediterranean*, 1997

Jewell, Helen, *Women in Medieval England*, Manchester University Press, 1996

Johnstone, Pauline, *Three Hundred Years of Embroidery, 1600–1900, Treasures from the Collection of the Embroiderer's Guild of Great Britain*, Wakefield Press, 1987

Kalavrezou, Ioli, *Byzantine Women and Their World*, Harvard University Press, 2003

Kemper, Rachel, H. *A History of Costume*, News Week Books, New York, 1979

Kerridge, Eric, *Textile Manufacturers in Early Modern England*, Manchester University Press, 1985

Kirshner, Julius & Wemple, Suzanne, *Women of the Medieval World, Essays in Honour of John H Mundy*. Basil Blackwell, 1985

Klapisch-Zuber, Christiane, Georges Duby & Michelle Perrot, ed, *A History of Women, Silence of the Middle Ages*, The Belknap Press of Harvard University Press, London, 1992

Knowles, David & R Neville Hadock, *Medieval Religious Houses in England and Wales* Longman, London, 1971

Kohler, Carl, *A History of Costume*, Dover Books, New York, 1963

Kolander, Cheryl, *A Silkworkers Notebook*, Interweave Press, 1985

Kurella, Elizabeth, *The Complete Guide to Vintage Textiles*, San Diego, 1999

Kybalova, Ludmila, *Coptic Textiles*, Paul Hamlyn, London, 1967

Labarge, Margaret Wade, *Women in Medieval Life*, Hamish Hamilton, London, 1987

Larousse Encyclopedia of Ancient & Medieval History, ed. Marcel Dunan, Paul Hamlyn, 1984

Larousse Encyclopedia of Byzantine & Medieval Art, ed Rene Huyghe, Paul Hamlyn London, 1968

Lattimore, Owen & Eleanor, *Silks, Spices and Empire, seen through the eyes of its discoverers*, The Great Explorers series, Tandem Books, 1973

Laver, James, ed. *Fashion, From Ancient Egypt to the Present Day*, Paul Hamblyn, London, 1967

Laver, James, *A Concise History of Costume*, World of Art Library, Thames and Hudson, 1979

Lawrence C H, *Medieval Monasticism*, Longmans, London, 1992

Le Coq, Albert von, *Buried Treasures of Chinese Turkestan*, Allen & Unwin, 1928

Le Goff, Jacques, ed *The Medieval World*, Collins & Brown, London, 1990

Le Ver de soie, BT Nature, 1994

Leyser, Henrietta, *Medieval Women, A Social History of Women in England, 450–1500*, Weidenfeld and Nicholson, London, 1995

Liu, Xinru, *Silk & Religion, An Exploration of the Material Life and the Thought of People. 600–1200*, Oxford University Press, Delhi, 1996

Loewe, Michael, *Everyday Life in Imperial China during the Han Period, 201BC–AD 220* Batsford, London, 1968,

Lofts, Norah, *Domestic Life in England*, Book Club Associates, 1976

Lopez, Robert S, and Erwing W Raymond, Transl. and Eds., *Medieval Trade in the Mediterranean World*, New York, Part of the Records of Civilization, Sources and Studies series.

Lucas, Angela M, *Women in the Middle Ages*, Religion Marriage and

Letters. The Harvester Press, Brighton, 1983

Mango, Cyril. *The Oxford History of Byzantium*, Oxford University Press

Marshall, Robert, *Storm from the East, From Genghis Khan to Khublai Khan*, BBC Books, London, 1993

Maxwell-Stuart, P G, *Chronicle of the Popes*, Thames &Hudson, London, 2006

Melling, J Kennedy, *Discovering London's Guilds and Liveries*, Shire Publications, 1981

Miller, Edward and John Hatcher, *Medieval England, Towns, Commerce and Crafts, 1086–1348. A Social and Economic History of England*, Longman, London & New York, 1995

Miskemin, *The Economy of Early Renaissance Europe*, 1300–1468

Mola, Luca, *The Silk Industry of Renaissance Venice*, Johns Hopkins

Money, D C, China, *The Land and the People*, Revised Edition, Evans Brothers, London, 1990

Monnas, Lisa, 'Opus Anglicanum and Renaissance Velvet: The Whalley Vestments', in *Textile History 25*, (1), 1994

Murowchick, Robert E, China, *Cradle of Civilization, Ancient Culture, Modern Land*, University of Oklahoma Press, 1994

Macartney, Lady, *An English Lady in Chinese Turkestan*, Oxford University Press, Hong Kong, Oxford, 1985

McEvedy, Colin, *The Penguin Atlas of Medieval History*, Penguin Books, 1984

Nicolle, David, *The Mongol Warlords, Genghiz Khan, Kublai Khan, Hulegu, Tamerlane*, Firebird Books, 1990

Nicolle, David, *The History of Medieval Life, A Guide to Life from 1000 to 1500AD*, Chancellor Press, 1997

Norris, Malcolm, *Brass Rubbing*, Pan Craft Books, 1965

Nunn, Joan, *Fashion and Costume 1200–1980*, The Herbert Press, London, 1985

Origo, Iris, *The Merchant of Prato*, The Reprint Society of London, 1959

Ormrod, W M, *England in the Thirteenth Century*, proceedings of the 1989 Harlaxton Symposium, Paul Watkins, Stamford, 1991

Paluden, Anna, *Chronicles of the Chinese Emperors, The Reign by Reign Record of the Rulers of Imperial China*, Thames & Hudson, 1998

Parker, Rozsika, *The Subversive Stitch, Embroidery and the making of the Feminine*, The Women's Press Ltd, 1984

Payne, Blanche, *History of Costume, From the Ancient Egyptians to the Twentieth Century*, Harper and Row, Publishers, New York, 1965

Peacock, John, *The Chronicle of Western Costume from the Ancient World to the Twentieth Century*, Thames & Hudson, 1991

Phillips, E D, *The Mongols*, Thames & Hudson, 1969

Pifferi, Enzo, *Como Citta della Seta*, 2001

Pisan, Christine de, *The Treasure of the City of Ladies, or The Book of the Three Virtues*, Penguin Classics, 1986

Planche, J R, *A History of British Costume, From Ancient Times to the Eighteenth Century*, Senate Reprint, 2001

Polo, Marco, *The Travels of Marco Polo*, Introduced by John Masefield, Dent London, Everyman's Library, 1975

Pound, N J G, *The Economic History of Medieval Europe*, Longman, 1988

Power, Eileen, *English Medieval Nunneries*, c1275 to 1535, Cambridge at the University Press, 1922

Power, Eileen, *Medieval People* Methuen London, Barnes & Noble, N.Y, 1963
Power, Eileen, *Medieval Women*, Folio Edition, 2001

Rawson, Jessica, *Mysteries of Ancient China*, New Discoveries from the early Dynasties, published by The Times, London
Rawson, Jessica, *Ancient China, Art and Archaeology*, Harper Row, 1980
Ribeiro, Aileen, *Dress and Morality*, B T Batsford, London, 1986
Ribeiro, Aileen & Valerie Cumming, *The Visual History of Costume*, Batsford, 1989
Rice, Tamara Talbot, *Everyday Life in Byzantium*, Batsford, 1967
Rice, David Talbot, *Constantinople, Byzantium, Istanbul*, Elek Books Ltd, London
Riley-Smith, Louise & Jonathan, *The Crusades, Idea and Reality 1095–1274*
Rowling, Marjorie, *Everyday Life in Medieval Times*, Carousel Books, 1973
Rutherford, Judith & Jackie Menzies, *Celestial Silks, Chinese Religious & Court Textiles*, Art Gallery of NSW, 2004

Sayles, G O, *The Medieval Foundations of England*, Methuen London, 1958
Schoeser, Mary, *World Textiles, A Concise History*, Thames & Hudson World of Art
Schoeser, Mary, *Silk*, Yale University Press, 2007
Scott, Margaret, *The History of Dress Series, Late Gothic Europe 1400–1500*, Humanities Press, New Jersey, 1980
Scott, Philippa *The Book of Silk*, Thames & Hudson, London, 1993
Sericulture Manuals, FAO 1: Mulberry Cultivation, 1995 2: Silkworm Rearing, 1995, 3: Silk Reeling, 1996
Silk & Rayon Uses Association, Incorporated, *The Silk Book*, London, 1951
Silk Manufacture, *A Treatise on the Origin, Progressive Improvement and Present State of the Silk Manufacture*, Longman's, London,
Simkin, C G F, *The Traditional Trade of Asia*, Oxford University Press, London, 1968
Sonwalkar, Tammanna N, *Hand Book of Silk Technology* New Age International (P) Limited, Publishers, 2001
Staley, Edgecumbe, *The Guilds of Florence*, Methuen, 1906
Staniland, Kay, *Embroiderers, Medieval Craftsmen*, British Museum Press, London, 1994
Stein, Marc Aurel, *Ruins of Desert Cathay, A personal Narrative of Explorations in Central Asia and Westernmost China.* in Two Volumes, Dover Publications Inc, NY
Synge, Lanto, *Antique Needlework*, Blandford Press, Poole, Dorset, 1982

Thompson, A Hamilton, *Bishop Alnwick's Visitation Records of Religious Houses in the Diocese of Lincoln*, Vol II, Pt 1, & 2, London, Canterbury & York Society, 1929
Thompson, Sally, *Women Religious, The Founding of English Nunneries after the Norman Conquest*, Clarenden Press, Oxford, 1991
Thorp, Robert L & Richard Ellis Vinograd, *Chinese Art & Culture*, Harry N Abrams, Inc, 2001
Thrupp, Sylvia, *The Merchant Class of Medieval London.* Ann Arbor, University of Michigan Press, 1962

Thubron, Colin, *Behind the Wall, A Journey Through China*, Heinemann, London, 1987

Uitz, Erika, *Women in the Medieval Town*. Barrie & Jenkins, London, 1990
Uitz, Erika, *The Legend of Good Women, The Liberation of Women in Medieval Cities*, Moyer Bell, 1994

Vaughan, Richard, trans & ed. *The Illustrated Chronicles of Matthew Paris*, Cambridge University Press, 1993.
Vengarde, Bruce L, *Women's Monasticism and Medieval Societies, England 890–1215*, Cornell University Press, 1997
Vainker, Shelagh, *Chinese Silk, A Cultural History*, British Museum Press, 2004
Virgoe, Roger, ed *The Illustrated Letters of the Paston Family, Private Life in the 15th Century*, Macmillan, London, 1989
Volbach, W Fritz, *Early Decorative Textiles*, Paul Hamlyn, London, 1969
Vollmer, Keall, Nagai-Berthrong, *Silk Roads: China Ships*, ROM, Toronto, 1983
Vollmer, John, *Silks for Thrones and Altars, Chinese Costumes and Textiles, From Liao through the Qing Dynasty*, published by Myrna Myers
Von Le Coq, Albert, *Buried Treasures of Chinese Turkestan*, Oxford University Press, Hong Kong, Oxford, New York, 1985
Vryonis, Speros, *Byzantium and Europe*, Thames & Hudson, 1970

Watson, William, Ancient China, *The Discoveries of Post Liberation Archaeology*, intro by Magnus Magnusson, BBC, 1974
Watt, James, CY, & Anne Wardwell, *When Silk was Gold, Central Asian and Chinese Textiles*, Abrams, US
Westwell, Ian, *China*, Chartwell Books, 2007
Whitelock, ed *English Historical Documents*, London, 1979
Whittock, Martyn, *The Pastons in Medieval Britain*, Heinemann, 1993
Whitfield, Susan, *Life along the Silk Road*, University of California Press, 1999
Wiesner, Merry E, Guilds, 'Male Bonding and Women's Work in Early Modern Germany', in *Gender and History* Vol 1 No 2 Summer, 1989
Willett, C & Phillis Cunnington, *Handbook of English Mediaeval Costume*, Faber, 1952
Williams, Marty & Anne Echols, *Between Pit & Pedestal, Women in the Middle Ages*, Markus Wiener, New Jersey, 1994
Wilson, Verity, *Chinese Dress*, Victoria &Albert Museum, Far Eastern Series, 2001
Wood, Frances, *The Silk Road, Two Thousand Years in the Heart of Asia*, The British Library, 2002
Wood, Frances, *Did Marco Polo go to China?*, Secker & Warburg, London, 1995

Yang, Sunny, Hanbok, *The Art of Korean Clothing*, HollyM, 1997
Yap, Yong & Arthur Cotterell, *The Early Civilization of China*, BCA, London, 1975
Yung, Peter, Xinjiang, *The Silk Road: Islam's overland route to China*, OUP, 1986

Index

A

Abbeys, Abbots, Abbesses, 66 68 70–1
Accessories, 85 105 108–10 115 125–132 135–137–8
Acre, 45–6
Acupictura, 64 75
Adam de Basing, 76–7
Afghanistan, 31 163
Africa, 39
Agents, 74–7 92 96
Alms, 85 116 132
Alamut, 50
Alexander the Great, 19 30–31 50
Alexandria, 30 34 164
Aliens, 99 106
Ambassadors, 56
Amber, 30
Animals, birds, 13 26 31 48 49 56 65 70 72–3 80 164–6
Antioch, 30–31 164
Apprenticeships 73–6 79 85–92 100–3 106–11 114–117 120
Arabs, Arabia, Arabic, 23 32 34 48 116 128
Aramaic, 27
Archbishops, 72–3 77–9
Arghun, 60–1
Aristotle, 19
Armenia, 31 46 48 165
Armour, 126 130 133
Asbestos, 30 54
Asia, 39
Assassin, 50
Astrology, 14
Attributes, 73 80

B

Babylonia, 20
Baby walker, 100
Bactria, 28–9 31 34
Baghdad, 39 45 48 163 165
Baku, 48 164
Baldach, 48
Bamboo, 14
Bandits, 25 30 38 164
Banners, 8 31 52–3 80 131
Barons, 54–6 166
Barbette, 126
Baron Ferdinand von Richthofen, 26
Battles, 31

Bave, Brin, 160
Bede, 66
Beguines, 114
Bezants, 54 56
Bible, 20 80
Bishops, 66 70–2 77
Black Death, 80
Black Prince, 134
Black Sea, 25 28 41 60 164
Bleaching, 153
Bliaut, 125
Blocking, 149
Bobbins, 114 143–8
Boccaccio, 33 84 157
Boileau, Etienne, 112
Bombyx mandarina Moore, 10 11
Bombyx mori, 12 141 143–5 150 155
Books, 59 122
Book of Sericulture, 8
Book of Trades, *Livre des Metiers*, 112
Bound feet, 59
Braid 65 74 85 88 111 141
Brais, 125
Brass, 124
Bribes, 21 27–8 34 164
Brocade, 31 39 48 53 104 119 165
Bronze, 12 13
Buddha, Buddhist, 18 25 53
Bukhara, 43 45
Burial, Sites, 12 30
Business, Businessmen 58 77 86–7 95–6 100–1 106–111 116 120
Buttons 88 95 110 132
Byzantium, 20 23 35 38–9 104 123 164

C

Camels, 26 29 39 59 63 164
Canterbury, 130–1
Caravans, 30 39 164,
Caravanserai, 26
Carding, Combing 150–7
Carpet, 48 56 167
Carpini, Giovanni di Piano, 42–3
Carriages, 59
Caspian, Plain, Sea, 28 36 43 48 50

Cave, 17 52
Caves of a Thousand Buddhas, 52–3 162–4
Caxton, 89
Central Asia, 20 25 30 34 42
Chainse, 125
Chancery Proceedings, 96 135
Chaperon, Chapeau bra, 86 125 132–6
Charity, Charities 108 110 128
Chasuble, 72–3 82–3 128
Ch'ang–an, 27 39
Chemise, 125 128 137–8
Children, 71 85 94 100 114 124 130 133
China, Chinese, 8–12 14–23 28–36 39–41 43 59–61 67 128 162–4
Chinchitalas, 54
Chivalry, 123
Christians, Christianity, 25 35 39 42–3 46 48 65 165
Christine de Pisan, 122
Church 20 22 36 42 45 65–6 71–3 79 81 85 94 104 106 110 119 123–4 128 132
Cinnamon, 30
Clare, 72–3 80
Cleaning, 124 133
Cleopatra, 30
Clergy, 36 70 73 131
Cloak, 125,
Cloth of Gold, 48 51 82 108 128 165–8
Cloth, Clothes, 29–32 35 71 85 108 123–124 128–38
Cluny, 82
Coal, 54
Coif, 125
Concubines, 56
Coleridge, Samuel Taylor, 54
Cologne, 104 116–119
Colour, 123
Confucius, Confucians, 15 25 29
Constantine, 35
Constantinople, 20 36 38 43
Contracts, 94
Cope, 72–4 78 130
Coral, 30
Corses, calles, 87–9 97 110
Cos, 19 33–4
Cosmetics, 137

Cote–hardi, Coat, 86 130–134
Couching, 65 73 78 82–3
Court, 8–16 20 94 98–9 104 109–10 123–4 130 134
Couvade, 58
Couvre–chef, 109 115
Crafts, craftsmen, 48 73 78 80 85–7 96 99 103–104 112 119–120 135
Crescent Lake, 63
Crespines, 105 132
Crimea, 41 43
Crusades, Crusaders, 39 41 50 80 123 126,
Cupping, 137
Currency, 16
Cushions, 129
Customs, 71

D
Dagging, 132 136
Damascus, 30
Death, 104 118 128 166
Debt, 90 93–5 106 111
Degummed cocoons 150 154
Deserts, 38 39 49 51–2
Designs, Designers, 65 67 72–3 78–82 130
Disease, Pests, 158–161
Dissolution, 78
Doge, 45
Dominicans, 46
Donors, 73
Doomsday book, 66
Doublet, 133–4 138
Dowry, 70
Drapers, 73 87
Dunhuang, 13 52 162–4
Durham, 67 73
Dyeing, Dyes, 8 12 34–5 38 65 78 96 117 133 140 151–5

E
Economy, 29 35
Education, 66 70
Egypt, Egyptians, 30 34 46 134
Embroiderers, Embroidery, 20 29 36–8 52–4 64–85 87 111 114–119 125 129 130 141 147 154–5 165–6
Empire, 20 28–31 34 36 38
Empress, Emperor, 8 15 18 20 32 37 56 125
England, 65 72 82 138 97 99
Erzurum, 48
Espionage, 21

Eunuchs, 56
Euphrates, 31
Europe, European, 22 39 41 43 125
Executrix, Executors, 88 108
Exporting, 59 87 96 98 117 167–168
Excavations, 88

F
Fabrics, 25–30 123
Fairs, 117–123
Family, 16 70–1 74 85–6 103 107
Fancy yarns, 149
Fardels, 11 96
Farmers, 16
Farthingale, 138
Fashion, Fashionable, 71 85 123–139
Feathers, 136
Felt, 54 155
Feme Couverte de Baron, Feme Sole, 92–4
Ferghana, 162
Finance, 117 120125
Fitch, Frannson, Ekwell, 76
Fitchets, 132 136
Flanders, 78
Florence, 39 106 116 119
Flowers, 13 82
Food, 16 52 70 85
France, 78 118 138
Fraternities, 100 104 110–111
French, Francesca, 52
Funeral, 59 124 166 168
Furnishings 80 124 126 129–130
Furs, Furriers, 30 46 54 58 73 102 105 108 125 127–127 139 166

G
Gansu, 14 162
Gaochang, 27
Garments, 117 123–130 142 154 166
Genoa 62 96 104 106 117
Gerogia, Georgians, 48 165
Ghelan, 48
Gifts, 15 29 42 58 60 73–7 85 100 128
Girdle, 86 88
Glass, 30,
Gloves 85
Gobi Desert, 25 28 51 162–4
Gold, Goldwork, Goldsmith, 31–32 35–8 42 46 48 56 65 72–82 85–7 97 105 108 111 116 123–4 129–130 134–136 148 165–7
Gospel of the Distaff, 112–113
Gossep, 87
Governments, 27 38 56 Gowns, 115 122 124 128 134 137–8 166
Great Wall, 28 59 162–4
Great Wardrobe, 78–9 96 101 110 124 128
Greece, Greek, 33–4 39 48 116
Groat, 54
Guilds, Guildsmen, 36 45 73 87 90–4 98 100–121 135
Gummy silk, 150 155
Gynaeceum, 11 22 36

H
Hagiographers, 68
Haberdashers, 87–8
Hair, 132 137
Hainaulters, 133
Handspun, 125 140 151–5
Han Dynasty, 16 29–30
Hansiatic League, 106
Hashish, 50
Hatchings, 158
Headdresses, Hats, 71 101–4 109 111 115 122 125 131–8
Heraldry, 80 117 131–2
Heden, Sven, 63
Hemp, 58 124
Hennin, 101–2 133 137–8
Hindu Kush, 25
Holy Family, 65 69
Holy Land, 29 41 50
Hose 86, 135–7
Hormuz, 49
Horses, 28 164
Houppleande, 95 105 122 127 135–7
Hygiene, 159

I
Illuminated manuscripts, 65
Imperial workshops, 22 30
Imports, 87 94–6 99 104 106 117
India, 16–17 22 28 30 32–6 48 60 158 163
Indus River, 24 25
Industry, 39 115 167
Instars, 158–161
Iran, 28 35 164
Iron, 16

INDEX *191*

Islam, 39
Italy, Italian cities, Italians, 41
   62 96 106 116 119

J
Jade, Gate, 13 30
Japan, 16–18
Jerusalem, 45
Jewels, 35–8 43 56 62 65 72–3
   78 88 108 123–6 137 166
Jews, Jewish, 23 25 116
Jiayuguan, 14 28
Journeymen, 107
Jupon, Jerkin, 80 133
Jures, 114–16,
Justinian, 20–21 37–8

K
Karakorum, 36 163
Kashgar, 51 162–4
Kashmir, 36 163
Kirtle, 67 86
Kerman, 48–50 165
Khans, 41–3 46 50 54–5 58–60
   166
Khanbalik, 43 45 56 58–9 166
Khotan, 14 18–19 22 51
Kings, 18 39 72–7 79 85 96–7
   99–100 104 106 110–12 115
   119 126–138
Kinsai, 59,
Kirtle, 115 125 135
Knights, 123 126 133–4 156
Knitting, 141 147–98 154
Korea, 16 17
Kublai Khan, 39 43–5 62
Kushan Empire, 28

L
Labour, 16 86 114
Lace, 88 97 99 110 132 141
Lady of the silkworms 6– 8
Lampas, 128 134
Langley, 70–2
Languages, 58
Latins, 48
Law, 95
Lebanon, 34
Levant, 39
Lombards, 98–9
   Leonard Conterin, 96
   Paul Penyk, 98
   Dyne Sanoche, 98
   Nicholas Sarduche, 98–9
Lo-tsun, 52
Liber Albus, 93
Linen, 20 30 78 86 118 124–5
   136
Liripipe, 136
Livery, 46 104 107–10
London, 78 85–104 106 111
   114 119–120 124 128 130
Long draw, 146 148
Lop Nor, 51 162 166
Loulan, 162
Loyang, 27
Looms, 12 13
Lucca, Lucchesse, 39 106 114
   116 129
Lustre, 142
Luttrell, 81
Lyon, 114 116 128

M
Mais Titianus, 27 Malaya, 34
Maniachis, 37–8
Manicheans, 25
Mantles, 125 131 134 139
Manufacturing, 58–9 115 150
   167
Manuscripts, 52–3 65 106 124
   133
Maps, 14 29 44
Markets, 26 98 109 123
Marriage, 66 85–6 92–5, 107–9
   131 139
Marseilles, 104
Martino da Canale, 45
Matthew Paris, 29
Mawata caps, Bells,
   Handkerchiefs, 150 154–5
Mayor & Aldermen 93–4,98,
   107–8
Medicine, 14 30
Medici, 108
Mediterranean, 30 39 41 45
   60 72
Mercers, 78 87 106–8
   Sir John Ffynkell, 94–5
Merchants, Adventurers 43 48
   58–9 74–5 78 85–7 94–6 100
   102–11 120 123 117 164–8
Merv, 36
Mesopotamia, 31 35
Metallic threads, 123 126 148
Metamorphosis, 20
Middle Kingdom, 15
Military, 29–30
Milk Street, 124
Milliners, 115
Ming, 39
Misogynism, 120
Missionaries, 25 43
Mistery, Mystery, 112

Mitres, 70
Modesty, Humility, 71
Mogao Caves, 52–3
Monasteries, 66 68 78
Money, coins, 16 54 167
Mongol, Mongolia, 42 46 48 58
Monks, 21–22 38 52
Morus alba, 10
Mosul, 48 165
Mourning, 134
Mt Ararat, 48
Mulberry, Trees, Leaves, Seeds,
   7–14 18 20 22 33 54 58
   158–161 167
Mulehet, 50
Mulier mercatrix sola, 110
Musicians, 56
Muslims, 25 39 41 48 50
Myths & Legends, 7 19–20 31
   34

N
Navigation, 35
Neolithic,12
Nestorians, 35 38 48
Net, 88
Nisibus, 35
Noil, 153
Nuns, Nunneries, Convents, 68,
   70–4 114

O
Oil, 48 142
Old Man of the Mountains,
   50–1 163
Opus Anglicanum, 66 72–3 80
Oracle bones, 13
Oriflammes, 80
Orphanages,114
Orphreys, 74
Ostriches, 30
Ottoman, 39
Outworkers, 86
Ovid, 20
Ovis Poli, 51

P
Pagan,59
Paintings, 124
Pakistan, 24 163
Palace, 56
Palermo, 39
Palestine, 45
Pall, 128
Paltok, 133–5

Pamirs, 25 26 50 162–4
Pamphile, 19 33 84
Paper, 14 54
Paris, 104
Parthians, 28 31 34–5
Paradise, 50
Parti–coloured, Parti–hose 132 135 139
Passports, 60
Paston, 96
Patterns, 36 38–9 80 147
Pausanius, 33
Payments, 74
Pearls, 30 37–8 73
Peasants, 16 125
Pelisson, 135–6
Persia, Persians, Gulf, 20 27–8 35 38 42 49 60–1 164–5
Petticoats, 118 138
Petitions, 98–9 106 112 120
Phoenicia, 34 38 164
Piece goods, 97
Pilgrims, Pilgrimages, 39 52 70
Pirates, 34
Plague, 103 124
Pliny, 19 32–3
Plying 142 146–9 153–5
Politics, 39 41 94 99 120
Polo, Marco, Nicolo, Matteo, 39–63 162–4 165–167
Pomander, 133
Popes, 39 41–2 45–6 60 70–2 77
Ports, 96
Portugal, 78 138
Postal service, 54
Pourpoint, 133
Power, 35 65 70 87 99 102–3 110–116,120
Procopius, 21, 38,
Prostitutes, 56 166
Prince, 60,
Princess, 18 22 60
Pseudomorph, 12
Pupa, Chrysalis, 158–161
Purple, 20 38 108
Ptolemy, 30

Q

Qin Dynasty, 23
Qing Dynasty, 9
Quilts, Quilting, 12 18 30 124 133
Queens, 67–8 70–9 110 122 126 130–9

R

Ravenna, 38
Raw silk, 58–9 86–8 96 98–9 104 117 168
Religions, 48
Rhubarb, 30
Ribbons 85 88 99 110 124–5
Robe, 74 134
Roman de la Rose, 138
Rome, Romans, 19 21 26 29–32 34–8 54 66
Rubruk, William, 42
Rule, 71
Russia, 30 42–3
Rusticello, 62

S

Sacred Eye, 11
Saints, 65–8 73 80–2
St Cuthbert, 67 73
St Louis, Fr 42
Salt, 16
Salerno, 116
Samarkand, 39 162–4
Samite, 108
Sanskrit, 23 52
Saracens, 39 41–2
Sarai, 43
Satin, 128 134
Saveh, 48
Scissors, 78
Sculpture, 124
Seamstresses, 79
Secondhand, 124
Secrets, 10 16 20 27 53 62 104
Seleucids, Seleucus, 31
Seres, Serica, Serinda, 21 23 27 30 34
Sericin, 8 9 11 152 154 155 158–161
Sericulture, 11–19 48 22 32 36 39 58 116 158–161
Servants, 16 111
Sewing silk, 96 110
Shakespeare, 20
Shang Dynasty, 12
Shang–tu, 54
Shantung, 14 59
Sheikh Alaodin, 50–1
Shield, 133
Ships, Boats, 34–6 43 44–5 49 60
Shoes, Poulaine, Cracows, 125 132 138–9
Shore, Jane 115
Sicily, 39

Sidon, 30
Silent trade, 27
Si Ling Shi, 6–8
Silk bricks, Slivers, Tops 150–1
Silk Carrier rods, 150 156
Silk cocoon, strippings, 7–14, 16 19 22 33 114 116 150–4 158–161
Silk fabrics, Textiles, 11–17 30 32 39 42 46 48 58–59 65 66–7 78 96 122–128 130–7 165–6
Silk Filament, Fibre, 19 143–6 150–5
Silk Floss, 16 29 78 85 150–2
Silk Garments, 37–8 42–3 56 58–9 71
Silk & gold 48 58–9 67–8 71–74 110
Silk Laps, Batts, 150 155
Silk–men, 85–8
 John Burton, 108
 Gerard Caniziani, 108
 Richard Claver, 87 92 95 107–8
 Thomas Fyler, 88
 David Galganete, 96
 William Horne 94
 Mertyns II Ume Hove, 117,
 Ralph Kemp, 108
 Johan Lambard, 102 115
 Condrad Louback, 117
 Peter Lutzenkirchen, 117–119
 Mertyn Neven, 117
 John Norlong, 108
 William Pratte, 87–9 106 108
 John Stokton, 87 108
Silk Moths, 158–161
Silk Paper, 13 152 155 167
Silk Road, Silk Route, 24–31 36 39–41 162–4
Silk Sliver, 142 151–2
Silk Thread, 16 56 67 78–9 88 116 130 143–7 167
Silk Thrums, 155
Silk–women, 85–103 106 117–120
 Elizabeth Atkynson, 92
 Elizabeth Bertram, 92
 Alice Bothe, 87–9
 Katherine Campion 100–1
 Alice Claver, 85 90–5 99–100 106 108–10
 Katherine Dore, 90
 Beatrix Fyler, 87 94 99
 Johanne Horne, 94
 Jane Langton, 96–7

Tryngen Louback, 117
Fygen Lutsenkirchen, 117–119
Lysbeth Lutzenkirchen, 117
Joan Marshall–Fyler, 88 99
Isabel Norman, 96
Marjery Rippyngale, 90
Elizabeth Stokton, 87 94 99 108
Margaret Tailour, 92
Joan Woulbarowe, 90
Silkworms, 8 14 19 33 84 152 158–161 167
Silkworm eggs, 8 18 21–22 158–161
Silver, 36 42 54 58 73 168
Singing Sands, 63
Skeining, 11 32 149–150
Slaves, 17
Slips 82–3
Sogdian, 52
Soldiers, 16 29
Solitary or Dry Tree, 60
Spain, 39 116–9 134
Spices, 30
Spiders, 34
Spinning, Spindles, Wheel, 12 66–7 73 85–91 111–16 128 141–152 156
Spitalfields, 104
Spun silk, 86 153
Stained Glass, 65
Staple, 151–2
State, 21 36 79
Status, 35 39 96 106 120 124
Stein, Sir Marc Aurel, 13 19 52 63
Steppes, 34 36
Stockings, 118
Stole & Maniple, 67 73
Strasbourg, 116
Sumptuary Laws, 118 124 128
Supertunic, 86 132
Surcoat, Surcote, 74 115 126 131 134–9
Symbols, 80 104
Syon cope, 64 78
Syria, 31 36–38

T
Tabas, 49
Tabard, 126 139
Tabby, 126
Tabriz, 48
Taffeta, 108 116 138
Tailors, 79 118–119 130 136
Taklimakan, 51 163

Tally sticks, 59
T'ang, 18 19 30
Taoists, Daoists, 25
Tapestry, 20 32 101
Tartars, 41–2 57 60 128
Tassels, 110
Tattooing, 58
Taxes, 15 16 21 27–8 34 38 112
Tea, 59
Tbilisi, 48
Tebaldo Visconti, 45–6
Temple of the Silkworms, 8
Tension, 145 154–5
Textiles, 68, 78
Thailand, 160
Toothpaste 133,
Theodora, 20,37–8,
Theophanes, 22
Three Magi, 37–8 48
Throw, Thrown silk, throwsters, 11 12 78 87–9 99–103 111 152 155
Tibet, Tibetan, 52 59–60
Tiepolo, Lorenzo, 45
Tiflis, 48 165
Tigris, 31
Tippets, 132
Tombs, paintings, bricks, 14 22 67
Trade, Traders, 15 16 21 25–28 34 36 39 41 43 48 58 85 89 94–5 100 103 108–12 117 128 162–4
Transport, 16 41
Travel, Travellers, 27 48 52 58–60 96 162–4
Treasure, Treasury, 20 52 32 35 77
Trebizond, 60
Tribute, 15 28–9 42
Truck system, 114
Tunics 108 125–6 131
Turkey, 39 48 167
Turkistan, 163
Turkomania, 48
Tussah, 39 144–5 150

U
Uighur, 52
Ungut, 56
Uzbekistan, 163

V
Veils, 71 104 132 136–8
Velvet, Veluti, 48 79 82 106 108 16 126 128 130–137
Venice, 39 40–3 45 60 62 96

104–7 110 117 128
Vestments, 36 68 71–73 78 80 128
Wimple, 67 132
Virgil, 199
Virgin Mary, 6 73 80
Visigoths, 35
Voltine, Mono, bi, Multi-voltine, 158

W
Wages, 29 79 86 90 92 107 114
War, 27 43 80 124
Warp, 147
Washing, 149–154
Waste silk, 153–155
Weather, 34
Wealth, 35 38 71
Weaving, Weavers, 8–18 32 34 36 38–9 84–5 88 104 106 116 119–121 124–5 140 165 168
Weigh, weighting, 9 49 81
Westminster Abbey, 129
Widows, 71 93–6 108–10
Wild silk, 19
William of Malmesbury, 68
Wills 88 95 108 111 124 128
Winchester, 124
Witchcraft, 112
Women, Work, 72 78–9 88 106 120,
Wool, woollen, 58 30 104 111 124 142 147 152
Workshops, 38–9 68 74 78–81
Writing, 13 23

X
X'ian, Chang'an 162–4
Xanadu, 54

Y
Yangzte, 10,12,
Yellow River 58,
York, 104,119,124,
Yuan Dynasty 55,
Yule, Henry, 62–3

Z
Zoroastrians, 25
Zurich, 116

www.ingramcontent.com/pod-product-compliance
Lightning Source LLC
Chambersburg PA
CBHW061928290426
44113CB00024B/2841